Post-Mao China and U.S.-China Trade

Post-Mao China
and U.S.-China Trade

Edited by Shao-chuan Leng

Published for
The Committee on Asian Studies
University of Virginia
by the
University Press of Virginia
Charlottesville

THE UNIVERSITY PRESS OF VIRGINIA
Copyright © 1977 by the Rector and Visitors
of the University of Virginia

First published 1977

Library of Congress Cataloging in Publication Data
Main entry under title:
Post-Mao China and U.S.-China trade.
   "An outgrowth of a symposium on U.S.-China trade that was held in Charlottesville, Virginia, on September 24 and 25, 1976, under the aegis of the Committee on Asian Studies of the University of Virginia."
   CONTENTS: Leng, S.-c. Introduction.—China, political and economic outlook: Scalapino, R. A. Perspectives on the People's Republic of China. Chen, N.-r. The Chinese economy in the 1970s.—Patterns and prospects of U.S.-China trade: Theroux, E.A. China's foreign trade. Dernberger, R. F. U.S.-China trade. [etc.] 1. United States—Commerce—China—Congresses. 2. China—Commerce—United States—Congresses. 3. China—Economic conditions—1949—Congresses. I. Leng, Shao Chuan, 1921—II. Virginia University. Committee on Asian Studies.
HF3128.P67   382'.0951'073   77-20811
ISBN 0-8139-0733-0

Printed in the United States of America

Contents

Introduction
Shao-chuan Leng

The passing of Mao Tse-tung and the subsequent purge of
the "Gang of Four" have ushered a new era in the People's
Republic of China. Peking's current emphasis on pragmatism
and economic development tends to give rise to high expectations of future trade between the United States and the
PRC as well as a move toward the normalization of their
relations. It is to the trade and other related issues
that the book addresses itself.

This volume is an outgrowth of a symposium on U.S.-
China trade that was held in Charlottesville, Virginia,
on September 24 and 25, 1976, under the aegis of the
Committee on Asian Studies of the University of Virginia.
The symposium brought together academicians and practi-
tioners (officials, businessmen, and lawyers) in a joint
endeavor to examine such questions of common concern as:

What is the role of trade in U.S.-China relations?

How significantly will the succession problem in
China affect its foreign and trade policies?

What has been Chinese foreign trade performance?

What are the prospects and problems of U.S.-China
trade?

What commodities are most likely to be exported
and imported, and what kinds of services may be in demand?

What type of trade with China is compatible with
the national interest of the United States?

How does one negotiate with the Chinese?

Can we separate trade from politics?

What are the relations of the China trade to the
international balance of power?

The essays contained in this volume are revised ver-
sions of the papers originally presented at the symposium.
Part I focuses its attention on the political and economic
outlook of China. In the opening essay Robert Scalapino
presents an analytical survey of the PRC based on the
recognition that Chinese political developments are "a
mix of personal factionalism and substantive issues."
In looking at the changing issues and institutions,
Scalapino discusses such concerns as the choice of a basic
economic model for China, the question of culture and
higher education, and the options within military, strategic, and foreign policy issues. In regard to the current
political scene, he analyzes the rivalry between the
Shanghai "radicals" and the "moderates" leading to the
victory of Hua Kuo-feng after Mao's death. He also talks
about the role of Teng Hsiao-p'ing, the fluctuations in
relative political influence of the military vs. the
Cultural Revolution faction, and the gap between rhetoric

and reality. In Scalapino's view, Mao has left behind him
weak institutions and powerful personalities, a combination
prone to unexpected changes and periodical upheavals. The
last section of the essay examines the future prospects of
China. While seeing little likelihood of the breakup of the
country, Scalapino suggests the possibilities of gradual
"de-Maoization" and of increasing professionalization of the
military. In addition, he discusses possible developments
in Chinese economy and higher education and in China's
foreign relations, especially with the Soviet Union and the
United States.
     In the following essay, Nai-ruenn Chen examines China's
economic policies, the performance and problems of major
economic sectors, some population and labor issues, and the
prospects of the future growth of China's economy. According
to him, China's primary economic goal is to become "a modern
economic power under socialism and with a high degree of
autarky." The current order of priorities is to develop
agriculture, then the light and heavy industry in that
sequence. However, Chen points out that the erratic development
of the Chinese economy since 1949 has shown clearly that
ideology and political campaigns cannot coexist with sustained economic growth. If the PRC is to achieve the goal
of evolving into a truly first-rate economic power by the
end of the century, he concludes, the post-Mao leadership
would have to discard, or at least greatly modify, some
aspects of Maoist ideology.
     Part II of the book deals with the patterns and pros-
pects of Sino-U.S. trade. It begins with Eugene Theroux's
survey of China's foreign trade, which is shown to be based
on two principles: (1) trade must be conducted on the
basis of equality and mutual benefit; (2) the purpose of
trade is to make China more self-reliant. Theroux cites
a couple of concrete examples to illustrate that Peking
does have an interest in and need for foreign advanced
goods and techniques but is reluctant to expand trade at
the expense of self-reliance. He then proceeds to examine
in detail China's foreign trade apparatus. Noting at the
outset that the PRC does not provide a climate hospitable
to investment and that foreign trade is a state monopoly
in China, Theroux discusses the structures and functions
of the Ministry of Foreign Trade, the Foreign Trade Corporations, collateral trade and related organizations, the
China Council for the Promotion of International Trade,
the Canton Fair, and other Chinese trade fairs. Finally,
he provides statistics for China's performance in foreign
trade.
     The next essay, by Robert Dernberger, is an appraisal
of U.S.-China trade and its future prospects on the basis
of the empirical evidence of the last five years. Referring to statistics and to his own estimates of 1969,

Dernberger offers the prediction that Chinese exports to the
United States will grow to about $400 million by 1980, with
a continued relative dominance of cotton fabrics and tin.
He is pessimistic about the likelihood of a significant
increase above that figure, even considering the possibility
of Chinese exports of oil to the United States or of China's
being granted most-favored-nation status. He further estimates that Chinese imports from the United States will grow
to 525 million current dollars of nonagricultural goods by
1980 but notes the difficulties of predicting the overall
volume of Chinese imports from the United States because of
such factors as fluctuations in Chinese domestic agricultural
production and political influence on China's trade decisions.
The author concludes that Sino-American trade will continue
to grow within his predictions but will not become a significant element of either country's total foreign trade. Nevertheless, this trade already has done well to "create an
initial, visible, and meaningful link between these two
countries in the new era of detente."

     Part III addresses itself to the political and other
aspects of China's foreign trade. The essay by Tao-tai Hsia
discusses China's foreign trade and the "Gang of Four."
He starts with an examination of various factors contributing
to the waning of China's foreign trade in 1976. He then
follows with an analysis of the alleged sabotage of foreign
trade by the Gang of Four as reported in official Chinese
sources. The volume, direction, and composition of the
PRC's trade are cited as three major issues in the debate
over foreign trade between the radicals and moderates among
the Chinese elites. Hsia ends his essay with an observation
on the prospects for China's trade under the Hua administration by taking into account even matters beyond its direct
policy on foreign trade.

     A very important aspect of China's trade potential,
its oil policy, is treated in the paper by Jerome A. Cohen
and Choon-ho Park. In their essay Cohen and Park review
developments that have occurred since they published a 1975
study that analyzed China's development into an oil exporter.
They emphasize the extent to which, in only two years, the
PRC's oil policy has come full circle, returning, after the
ouster of the Gang of Four, to an export strategy that
seeks to earn at least relatively modest amounts of foreign
exchange for financing capital imports necessary for rapid
economic growth. Although the authors agree with the Hua
Kuo-feng government's claim that the opposition of Mao's
widow and her comrades did indeed adversely affect that
strategy during 1976, they also evaluate a variety of other
factors that promise to limit China's prospects for becoming
a significant oil exporter. They conclude that despite
the recent setbacks to China's economy in general and to
oil production in particular, the People's Republic can

still be expected to increase oil exports during the next
decade, especially to Japan, but that China is not going to
become a major oil exporter. While its exports will prove
politically beneficial in solidifying China's relations
with Japan, they will not be so large as to give the PRC
undue influence over that important country.

The final essay of the volume, by Ralph Clugh, is on
the international impact of China's foreign trade. He
begins with an assessment of China's economic impact on
countries for which it is a major trading partner. He
also examines whether the PRC poses a serious problem to
countries exporting similar products. The major part of
the essay consists of two detailed studies of the political effect of the PRC's foreign trade. The first, on
Japan, is an account of how the PRC has tried to maniuplate
its trade with Japan for political gains. One example is
how Japanese business delegates have sometimes agreed to
China's political conditions for trade, including strong
criticisms of their own government. A similar account is
given of the political impact of China's trade on West
Germany, Canada, and, peripherally, Australia. In his
concluding observation, Clough suggests that the international impact of China's trade could increase substantially
only if the post-Mao leadership should decide to rely on
foreign trade to speed Chinese economic development.
However, increasing involvement in international trade,
he further states, would likely make the Chinese hesitant
to manipulate trade for political ends because of the
high economic costs entailed.

It is not possible to include in this volume the contributions of all participants in the U.S.-China Trade
Symposium. Nor was an attempt made at the conference to
present any conclusions. However, there was a common
expectation that economic exchanges between the PRC and
the United States would continue to expand along with
further development of their political relations in the
post-Mao era. At the same time it was generally recognized
that given some inherent economic and political constraints,
the growth of Sino-American trade would be rather limited
in scope even with the normalization of relations between
the two countries. The sensitive question of technology
transfers was also examined in the deliberations. Many
participants felt that in the context of a continuing
Washington-Peking detente the United States should sell
to the PRC technology and equipment that could be used
for civilian as well as defensive purposes, e.g., certain
types of computers and transport jets. As to direct
American arms sales to China, the prevalent opinion
suggested caution in view of possible repercussions in
Asia and the Soviet Union.

The convening of the symposium and publication of this volume were made possible by financial contributions from Ethyl Corporation, Fitzgerald & Company, Philip Morris International, Universal Leaf Tobacco Company, the Alice Leng Memorial Fund, and the Ellen Bayard Weedon Foundation. Thanks are due to the cooperation and assistance of Ronald Dimberg, Frederick Nolting, Yee-ling Rothman, C. Stewart Sheppard, and William Weedon. Special appreciation goes to Fitzgerald Bemiss and Alfred Fernbach for their valuable advice and support.

PART I

China: Political and Economic Outlook

1.   Perspectives on the People's Republic of China

Robert A. Scalapino

On November 1, 1976, the official organ of the Chinese Communist Party, Jen-min jih-pao, headlined a report, "Overthrow of 'Gang of Four' Leads to Victory in Production." The report proclaimed that as a result of "the great revolutionary drive displayed by the workers" after the appointment of Hua Kuo-feng as chairman of the Party Central Committee and the Military Commission, and "the great historic victory in smashing the plot of the 'gang of four' to usurp party and state power," rapid increases in Peking's chemical factory production had taken place.[1]

It is noteworthy that similar productive increases in various fields were announced in conjunction with the ouster and discrediting of Teng Hsiao-p'ing (at a time when the so-called Left controlled the media), and even earlier, in the aftermath of the startling Lin Piao incident. If one takes these reports seriously, a new dialectic can be discerned. Every political crisis results in improved worker morale and major productive gains. Thus, political upheaval and economic development go hand in hand.

In that event, there should have been no shortage of economic advances in recent years, for China has been surfeited with political changes affecting the top political and military elite. In one sense, to be sure, the struggle for power within the Chinese Communist Party has been a consistent aspect of its entire history. Yet when that party achieved power over the whole of China in 1949, unity at last seemed the order of the day. Mao Tse-tung had attained unchallengable supremacy, with such loyal lieutenants as Chou En-lai, Liu Shao-ch'i, and a host of veteran military figures grouped around him. The "international faction," most closely aligned with Moscow, had been relegated to secondary roles, but all of its living members were included in the fold. Thus, the party entered its era of power with factional struggles seemingly behind it, more united than at any point in the recent past.[2]

This unity was generally preserved during the first years of the new order. Two leaders, Kao Kang and Jao Shu-shih, were purged for "mountaintopism" in 1954, charged with having set up their own independent kingdom and plotting to challenge the center. This was an exceptional event, however. Not until the ill-fated Great Leap Forward, which opened in late 1957 and had already run into trouble by 1958, did serious divisions within top leadership ranks develop, signaled most clearly by the ouster of P'eng Te-huai and his close associates in 1959.[3]

The retreat of Mao from the policymaking front line, the rise of the Liu-Teng team who together with Chou En-lai sought to modify the excesses of the Great Leap, and the emergence of Lin Piao as a key military-political figure marked the complex developments of the early 1960s.   This was the period during which the seeds of the Great Proletarian Cultural Revolution were planted, with preliminary skirmishes on the educational and cultural fronts, pitting Peking intellectuals (with party support) against Mao's wife, Chiang Ch'ing, her Shanghai supporters, and that indispensable personage, Mao himself.   To this group was added Lin Piao and through him, powerful elements (although not the entirety) of the military.

To summarize recent political events in China with such an emphasis upon personalities, however, is to signal one of the most critical problems faced by the analyst of the contemporary Chinese scene.   In the mix of personal factionalism and substantive issues, what weight should be given each?   Have the great upheavals characterizing Chinese politics in the past two decades been essentially the product of the personal rivalries and struggles for power among a group of aging men (and women) who have known each other too well, too long?   In broader terms, are there elements in Sinic culture, deeply imbedded in the traditions of this society and surviving Communism, that promote a particular type of factionalism derivative from the small group and its unique behavioral patterns?   Moreover, have these traits been accentuated in the era just past by virtue of the fact that the first generation of Communist leaders were predominately rural in their antecedents, coming from the middle and upper peasantry, growing up in suburban environments that were near, but not of, China's cities?

Before assigning a clear priority to personal factionalism in assessing Chinese politics, one must consider the environment in which the politics of this extraordinary society has operated, including the changing nature of both institutions and issues.   One faultline of significance can be fixed in 1954, the year during which the new constitution of the People's Republic of China came into effect.   With this event, the growing division of labor characterizing the Communist elite since its guerrilla days was given additional impetus, being institutionalized in relatively fixed form.   Functional differentiation meant the emergence of bureaucratic interest-group politics in China as elsewhere, with the party, the administrative state organs and the military each being affected.

Meanwhile, new challenges emerged in the form of issues complex in nature, massive in implication, and difficult if not impossible to resolve in a manner satisfying to all.   What were these issues?   One with profound implications, both for domestic and foreign policy, was the question of what basic economic model was appropriate

for China. The initial emphasis was upon the development
of heavy industry, with extensive Soviet support. Such a
program was critical if China were to obtain the type of
independence demanded by the nationalist-Communist leaders.
Yet it was soon recognized that the Soviet forced march
toward industrial preeminence had come via policies that
sternly limited investment in agriculture and provided
scant opportunities for self-improvement on the part of the
peasants. With at least four hundred million peasants,
many of whom lived at the marginal level of survival,
pressing upon China's already densely packed cities, would
a similar program not produce the most serious socio-
economic and political consequences?

Chinese agricultural gains during the early 1950s were
not inconsiderable, product in part of the end of incessant
conflict, in part of the massive use of corvée labor on
water conservancy and irrigation projects. Yet the gap
between the rural and urban sectors threatened to grow
wider at a rapid rate. At root, the commune system was
an effort to answer this problem.[4] The commune was to
represent a larger, more efficient administrative unit,
one in which production could be effectively maximized,
and consumption carefully controlled. It was also attuned
to a program of bringing small- and medium-scale industry
to the countryside. This industry, while poorly capitalized
and relatively primitive, could take advantage of cheap
and plentiful manpower to make the rural areas more self-
sufficient (hence less of a drain on the urban sector)
and more modern. In this aspect of the program, the evidence of earlier Japanese experience was much stronger
than that of the Soviet model. An additional aspect of
agrarian policy was the "down to the countryside" movement, whereby millions of youth were transferred from urban
to rural areas after middle school graduation, with the
idea of alleviating urban underemployment and infusing the
hinterland with low- and middle-level technology. Some
twelve million youth had been transferred by 1976.

Thus, in recent years, the slogan has been "Agriculture
as the foundation; industry as the leading factor." No
such far reaching program could have been inaugurated and
sustained without controversy, particularly since it was
initiated with record speed. Collectivization ran against
peasant instincts and desires in a most profound manner,
and the question of the role of private plots has been a
perennial problem, along with other aspects of the incentive issue. The size of the commune and the central locus
of decisionmaking within the commune have also been matters
often debated. Nor have the broader questions of state
investment to agriculture versus industry been easily or
permanently resolved. And extensive resistance to the "down
to the countryside" movement has been acknowledged by the
government.

Other issues in the economic realm have also been of importance. Problems relating to planning and the management system are endemic to a socialist state. Is the emphasis to be upon a professional managerial system or extensive worker control? What shall be the mix between centralized planning and decentralized decisionmaking? How much weight shall be given to economic incentives in the industrial sector? Is "self-reliance" to be the central objective, and how is this to be achieved, both at local and national levels? Around all of these issues, controversies have swirled, with shrill rhetoric often invoked. Not infrequently, moreover, high officials have fallen in these battles, charged with being "capitalist roaders," or similar crimes.

Controversy has not been limited to the econimic realm. Indeed, the most visible issues of the last decade have pertained to culture and higher education.[5] The Cultural Revolution was intended to wipe out those traditional art forms "conducive to reactionary thought," substituting "revolutionary opera" and other ideologically laden, policy-oriented forms of creative expression. Socialist realism was the order of the day. But critics, reportedly including Teng Hsiao-p'ing, sarcastically derided the new art, noting that "opera tickets do not seem to be selling well these days!"

It has been in the field of higher education, however, that the most sensitive nerve ends of the combatants in the political arena have been touched. On the one side, the charge has been leveled that since the Cultural Revolution, China's higher educatonal system has been "a mess," with quality sacrificed in favor of admitting individuals solely on the basis of political criteria, thus turning colleges and universities into institutions for remedial education and jeopardizing China's future growth and security. With the curriculum heavily politicized, student capacities at a low level, and graduate studies largely in abeyance, from whence will come China's future scientists, engineers, and other high-level technicians?

The answers to these charges have been vituperative if not wholly satisfactory. The old order, it is asserted, sustained a bourgeois intellectual elite, one that disdained physical labor and sought education in order to become officials. Thus, China's educational system prior to the Cultural Revolution undermined socialist goals, maintained reactionary class attitudes, and--in a more practical sense--graduated individuals who could not adequately be employed. The first need was for lower- and middle-level technology on a wide front, namely, better trained peasants and workers. The pre-1966 system led to revisionism and the corrupt Soviet patterns. Put politics in command, and the masses will exhibit the creativity necessary for both the ideals and the goals of Communism.[6]

In its essentials, this debate centers upon the struggle between "revolution" and "development." These two forces, to be sure, are not invariably at odds. When formidable obstacles need to be swept away, revolution may aid development. But when ideological purity threatens to interfere with quality, reject complexity, and view with suspicion the very concept of intellectualism, then revolution can become antidevelopmental. And this confrontation has existed recently in China, understandably perhaps, given the conservative anti-urban, anti-intellectual background of many of China's senior revolutionaries, including Mao Tse-tung.

Yet another realm of controversy has existed over military and strategic issues.[7] Should China's basic strategy rest upon the concept of "people's war," supplemented by a limited but growing nuclear arsenal? Is the prospect of facing millions of civilian militia, defending every foot of Chinese soil, sufficient to deter any potential aggressor, particularly if a capacity for some degree of nuclear retaliation exists? It should be recognized that irrespective of the military merits of such a strategy, its political implications cannot be ignored. At what point does a strong militia become a competitor with the professional army, and a potent political instrument among the contestants for power? The available evidence strongly suggests that this has been a rising issue in the recent past. There are factors, moreover, that argue for greater attention to the modernization of China's conventional military forces--land, sea, and air--and one may be certain that a number of professional military men have made that case.

Inextricably connected with some of the above issues are matters of foreign policy. Here, relations with the Soviet Union are central to all other questions. Did Mao and his cohorts go too far in antagonizing the Soviet Union, thereby inducing high risks and limited flexibility for the People's Republic of China? Could continued Russian assistance have supported China's needs, both in the military field and in the realm of economic modernization? Or is it in the interest of the PRC to promote security as well as economic ties with the non-Communist world, especially with Japan, Western Europe, and the United States?

To many of the issues set forth above we shall later return. This survey, however, should suffice to indicate that the range of concerns--and controversies--steadily widened in the tumultuous years after 1956. Certainly, one cannot rule out the effect of these issues upon the cleavages within Chinese politics that subsequently occurred. In establishing the mix between personal factionalism and differences over substantive issues, we may assume that the ratio has been neither constant nor susceptible to a clear-cut delineation. Undoubtedly, both personal and institutional

ties produced proclivities toward certain positions on
the issues under consideration, and on occasion, the proclivities derived from these two ties may have been in
conflict. In any case, the substantive stands taken may
often have exacerbated personal rivalries, granting that
over the entire political arena the paramount question of
power allocation hung, persistent and unyielding.

In such a setting, "loyalty" and "betrayal" become
vital and often unpredictable elements in the political
equation. Irrespective of past positions and personal
views on the issues at hand, if the immediate question
narrows down to that of survival or oblivion, of "supporting Chairman Mao" or "remaining with the forces of reaction," how many individuals are prepared to march straight-
forwardly to their political doom? Will not the tempta-
tion to "confess past mistakes" and denounce "those who
led me astray" be overwhelming, especially if redemption
is promised?

Chinese politics in recent years have borne a strong
resemblance to the court politics of an aging dynasty.
Intrigue has been omnipresent among those vying for the
favor of the old emperor, with repeated charges of plots
and counterplots. Favorites have been summoned, honored,
and not infrequently, then disgraced. Provincial loyalties
have seemed to vary, a matter of deep concern in Peking,
with emissaries from the center being regularly dispatched
to straighten matters out. And the women of the inner court,
especially the empress, have played important, sometimes
crucial roles. In contrast to earlier times, however, it
is a court that has been very cognizant of the importance
of the mobilized masses. Hence, control of the armed
forces, the party apparatus, and the media has been at the
heart of the contest, for these are the indispensable
instruments of power in a Communist state.

Taking the perspectives advanced thus far, how should
we analyze the current political scene in China, and assess
future prospects? Today, China is governed at the top by
a coalition of very senior party-administrative cadres
and professional military men. With a few prominent exceptions, this is now a group whose importance predates the
Cultural Revolution and who in some cases were adversely
affected by it. Hua Kuo-feng, now China's top leader, is
one of the exceptions. While Hua himself is a relatively
senior cadre, his national prominence stems from the
Cultural Revolution and presumably from his longtime
association with Mao's native province, Hunan, and the
chairman's substantial personal support. Hua is also
young in comparative terms, being approximately fifty-six.
His specialization in agriculture and the fact that his
leadership in commune development took place in such a
strategic region (Mao's native <u>hsien</u>) have undoubtedly

stood him in good stead. Hua's rise prior to the dramatic
events of 1976 was signaled by his appointment as minister
of public security, a post of great sensitivity and power.
It is inconceivable that he could have occupied this position without being acceptable to most if not all major
elements in the political arena, including Mao. Indeed,
it is currently believed that Hua's replacement of Teng
Hsiao-p'ing was a compromise, acceptable at the time to
both "moderates" and "leftists."

     To use these latter terms in connection with Chinese
politics is convenient but hazardous. It implies a neat
two-fold division throughout the political structure that,
if not wholly misleading, is at least too precise. As we
have noted, the mix between personal factionalism and
positions on substantive issues is, in all probability, a
highly complex and shifting one. On a number of the issues
outlined earlier, the differences between moderates and
leftists range along a continuum rather than being sharply
dichotomized. On some issues, indeed, a consensus may exist.
Over every aspect of the scene, moreover, a major gap
between rhetoric and reality exists, with the rhetoric
vastly "harder" and more pure than the actual conditions.
Imbedded in Chinese political culture is a seeming capacity
to rest comfortably with this dichotomy, as if the very
statement of a goal or principle is in some measure a
substitution for its achievement.

     After these caveats and modifications have been set
forth, however, it remains a fact that those individuals
known recently as the Shanghai Group, and now labeled the
"Gang of Four," namely, Chang Ch'un-ch'iao, Chiang Ch'ing,
Wang Hung-wen and Yao Wen-yüan, flew leftist banners in
their quest for power. Dominating the media, they sought
to continue the main themes of the Cultural Revolution,
notably, those of "putting politics in command," down-
playing "expertise" and "economic-firstism." Thus, they
were quick to attack those accused of being attuned to
pragmatic, incentive-oriented policies as "capitalist
roaders." Moreover, aligned with "radical" students and
cadres, they appear to have been in the vanguard of the
support for the post-Cultural Revolution higher education
system, denouncing those who wanted to improve the quality
of that system by restoring scholastic criteria for
admissions and reintroducing graduate training together
with more basic research.

     It also seems likely that they hoped to create a power
base in the people's militia, offsetting to some extent
their weak links with the People's Liberation Army.
Probably they strongly supported efforts in the aftermath
of the Lin Piao incident to reduce the power of the military
within the party and the administrative structure, both
at provincial and national levels. Presumably, also,

they looked with apprehension as Teng Hsiao-p'ing and others rehabilitated and brought back into active service a number of senior cadres earlier humiliated and purged in the course of the Cultural Revolution.

Increasingly, the evidence points to the fact that their most formidable opponent until his death was Chou En-lai, but Chou by virtue of his political adroitness remained untouchable. Mao--whatever may have been his doubts at certain points (and in the aftermath of their purge, these are probably being greatly exaggerated)--was their chief benefactor and source of power. Thus, their authority was hinged to personal, not institutional, ties despite the fact that they were catapulted into the highest offices, rising like helicopters, to use Teng's derisive phrase. In his final months, Mao may also have been their prisoner, since they increasingly controlled access to him and could therefore speak and write in his name.

To illustrate the importance of these facts it is essential to explore the political situation within China at the point of Mao's death in broader terms. Perhaps, as is now asserted, Mao himself proposed Hua for the posts of first vice-chairman of the party and premier of the state to succeed Teng in April 1976 and later gave him additional personal backing. It must be remembered, however, that on at least two earlier occasions, Mao had seemingly chosen his heirs with great care, only to repudiate them later. The fate of Liu Shao-ch'i and Lin Piao illustrates how dangerous was the position of Number Two in late Maoist China. To the list might be added Teng Hsiao-p'ing, although the precise relation between Mao and Teng in recent years is not clear. It must be assumed that Teng's restoration and his assumption of all the key posts under Mao was essentially the work of Chou En-Lai, then dying with cancer. It must also be assumed that Mao approved. Indeed, we know that he signaled Teng as his probable successor to high American authorities at one point. But Teng, in addition to being burdened with certain indiscretions that were a part of his personality, was clearly anathema to those who had engineered the Cultural Revolution. Both his policies and his personal ties represented overt challenges.

Possibly Teng appealed initially to Mao as a man who could control the military, and in the aftermath of the Lin Piao affair, it was clear that the military constituted a potential threat. At the close of the Cultural Revolution, the Communist Party of China was the most highly militarized party of its type in the world. Among the Eighth Central Committee members first appointed in 1956, more than one-half had been "overthrown" in the course of the Cultural Revolution, the great majority of them veteran party-administrative cadres, high in rank and

seniority. In the Ninth Central Committee, created in
April 1969 after the chaotic events of the previous three
years, military men currently on active duty constituted
some 45 percent of the total membership, with mass representatives 28 percent, and party-administrative cadres
representing only 27 percent.[8]
    This same pattern was exemplified even more extensively
as the party was reconstructed in 1970-71 at the provincial
level. Approximately two-thirds of the provincial party
full secretaries were professional military men initially,
compared to the party-administrative cadres who constituted
28 percent, and the mass representatives with only 5 percent. Substantial sections of China were in fact under
martial law, with the military in control at all levels.
    A similar distribution prevailed at the top of the
political structure. Of the twenty-five full members of
the Ninth CC Politburo, eleven were professional military
men as against fourteen party-administrative cadres and
mass representatives.[9] At the uppermost level, the Standing
Committee of the Politburo, stood five veterans--Mao
surrounded by "his close comrade in arms," Lin Piao; the
indispensable Chou En-lai; longtime "theorist" Ch'en
Po-ta, who was once secretary to Mao and completely dependent upon his favor; and a man whose career was associated
with "public security" work, K'ang Sheng. Today, all of
these men are gone--Lin and Ch'en having been purged;
Mao, Chou, and K'ang removed by death.
    The first major changes took place in the autumn of
1971, although Ch'en Po-ta fell earlier. Lin Piao, his
wife, and a group of close military associates were accused
of planning a coup d'etat, involving the assassination of
Mao. It is very possible that we will never know the full,
accurate story of this affair. Even the question of whether
Lin and other "plotters" died in the Mongolian crash of a
PLA plane is debated, although Chou En-lai and others have
asserted flatly that this was the case, and there has been
no strong contradictory evidence to date.[10]
    In any case, it is clear that within months after the
Ninth Party Congress of April 1969, the top elite of the
nation were in deep disarray, with some of the most powerful military-political figures grouped around Lin Piao,
determined to make certain that Mao's succession went in
their direction. Once again, personal factionalism in
connection with the power struggle and substantive issues
were intermeshed. From various sources, including official
ones, we learn that the Lin group charged the Mao-Chou
regime with a number of errors and crimes, reflective of
the substantive issues noted earlier. The economy had
allegedly bogged down, with living standards depressed and
the vast masses of the peasantry suffering. The freezing

of wages for factory labor was attacked as a form of exploitation, and the "down to the countryside" movement was
defined as "labor reform in disguise." It was asserted that
the Red Guards had been manipulated and turned into cannon
fodder during the Cultural Revolution, and subsequently made
scapegoats. Mao, moreover, was called a "great feudalistic
tyrant," another Chin Shih Huang (the first emperor of the
Chin dynasty).

The demise of Lin Piao and his group had two short-range
results in political terms. First, the Shanghai Group--
those who had shot upward with Mao's protection as vanguard
leaders of the Cultural Revolution--advanced still further,
with a young man, Wang Hung-wen, unknown at the outset of the
Cultural Revolution, skyrocketing to a position next to Mao
and Chou, becoming vice-chairman of the Party and Military
Commission. Chang Ch'un-ch'iao also assumed key posts in
the party, state administration, and military. Both men were
advanced to the Standing Committee of the Politburo, with
Mao's wife, Chiang Ch'ing, and her protégé, Yao Wen-yüan,
joining them at a slightly lower level as full members of
the Politburo.

A second development was also made manifest. The military, having proved to be a serious threat, now came under
the closest scrutiny, with actions taken to reduce military
power in party and state organs. Thus, when the Tenth Party
Congress was held in August 1973, the Politburo which was
elected contained only two military men on its Standing
Committee--Yeh Chien-ying and Chu Te, two individuals long
separated from active command and greatly advanced in years.
Among the full and alternate members of the new Politburo,
however, a sufficient number of active military men remained
to signal the continued importance of this category. Three
key military commanders--Ch'en Hsi-lien, Hsu Shih-yu, and
Li Te-sheng--were accorded full membership in addition to
Hua Kuo-feng, now minister of public security. To this group
should be added Su Chen-hua, deputy commander of the navy
and new Politburo alternate member.

In truth, throughout this period the military was no
more united than other elements on the political scene.
Many events--beginning with the purge of Peng Te-huai and
coming to a climax with the Cultural Revolution--had served
to drive deep wedges at all levels, with older factional
alignments palying their full role. Thus, as one or more
factions went down, others gained opportunities to move
ahead.

The new Tenth Central Committee of 1973 sustained the
trends revealed in the Politburo. The percentage of military cadres among full and alternate members dropped from
44 to 31 percent. On the other hand, those who could be
considered to have been in the vanguard of the Cultural
Revolution rose from 28 percent (in the Ninth CC) to

36 percent (in the Tenth CC), with the veteran party-
administrative cadres increasing by only 1 percent, to
28 percent. Once again, the military remained extremely
important, representing nearly one-third of the total
membership in this, the party's vital national organ.
The ascendancy of the so-called Cultural Revolution faction, however, was striking, a fact that in the final
analysis could only be attributable to Mao's support.[11]

In December 1973, a further action was taken to
reduce military influence. A major reshuffle of military
region commanders was executed, with eight of the eleven
commanders shifted to other regions, and for the most
part, divested in their provincial party and administrative roles. It soon became clear, moreover, that this
was part of a broader effort to reduce the military quotient in provincial party and state organs. Throughout
the 1974-75 period, transfers continued, with the number
of military men on the political roles dropping. By the
latter part of 1975, the number of military men serving
as provincial party full secretaries had been reduced to
74, or 47 percent, from the 82, or 66 percent, of 1970-71.
Party-administrative cadres, on the other hand, had risen
from 35 (28 percent) to 68 (43 percent), with mass representatives going from 6 (5 percent) to 16 (10 percent)
Once again, while the trend was apparent, the continued
importance of the military in Chinese politics could not
be denied. In any future crisis, the military were almost
certain to play a crucial role.

It was also clear that this was likely to be the
Achilles' heel of the Shanghai Group, since their military
support seemed strictly limited, particularly after the
split from Lin Piao. As noted earlier, it is possible
that a principal reason for the acceptability of Teng
Hsiao-p'ing to Mao and the radicals lay in his longtime
connections with the military, and the belief that he could
be extremely useful in the drive to reduce military power
within party and administrative circles. It should be
remembered that he was rehabilitated in the spring of 1973,
prior to the military reduction campaign, and elevated
to the Politburo in January 1974, just after the personnel reshuffle in the military regions.

In any case, another route was being pursued during
this period, namely, a buildup of the people's militia.
Wide publicity in particular was being given the Shanghai
people's militia, with the suggestion that it should be
a model. Leadership of the militia was different from
that of the People's Liberation Army, and earlier, the
public security forces had also been put under separate
jurisdiction. The implications of these various developments could not have escaped the attention of key PLA leaders, who, however divided among themselves, must have had
apprehensions.

In politics, it is important to know when to die. The passing of Chou En-lai prior to Mao, on January 8, 1976, triggered the events that immediately followed. Almost certainly, if Mao had preceded Chou in death, Teng's tenure in office would have continued, at least for a certain period. With their most powerful opponent gone, however, the radicals zeroed in on Teng, using a range of charges against him that once again revealed various cleavage lines over important substantive issues. Teng, to be sure, had not helped his cause by a boldness of speech and an arrogance of manner. His support among the military, moreover, may have been weakened as a result of the actions taken under his premiership to reduce the military reach. And access to Mao may have become increasingly difficult, with the basic controls exercised by his wife and her closest cohorts.

Whatever the intrigue surrounding this period, the attack upon Teng, as it was displayed before the masses, bore a strong leftist imprimatur. Cast in ideological terms, the central charge was that Teng, by emphasizing unity and production, was relegating the class struggle to a secondary position, thereby undermining the dictatorship of the proletariat. Invoking Mao, the attackers proclaimed the class struggle "the key link," and asserted that the struggle between two lines would continue for the indefinite future. There would be other persons like Wang Ming, Liu Shao-ch'i, and Lin Piao. Thus, the fight against the bourgeoisie had to take place within the party as well as elsewhere. Indeed, in Teng yet another "capitalist roader" was to be found, a renegade who despite his earlier promises had once again proved to be a faithful servant of the reactionary classes.

The specific charges against Teng are some indication of the issues of the day, and once again reflect the unresolved legacies of the Cultural Revolution. In addition to denigrating the new opera, Teng had launched a frontal assault upon the post-Cultural Revolution educational system. Nor were the charges less serious in the economic realm. Teng reportedly had questioned the decentralization measures undertaken during the Cultural Revolution, and favored a restoration of managerial over worker control in the factories. At every turn, moreover, he had sought to increase economic incentives, thereby pursuing the revisionist, capitalist line. No charges against Teng were made in the arena of foreign policy, but on the domestic political front he was accused of having sought to "restore hermits properly consigned to oblivion," a thrust at his policy of rehabilitating many veteran cadres.

By April 1976 Teng had been removed from all of his posts and once again had become a nonperson. In his

place, Hua Kuo-feng had emerged. When offered the position, Hua reportedly demurred at first, claiming that he
was not sufficiently qualified, a response perfectly in
accordance with traditional Chinese political etiquette.
The Politburo Standing Committee was now reduced to five
members: Mao and the two Shanghai Group leaders, Wang and
Chang, the aged but powerful Yeh Chien-ying, and Hua himself. Chou, K'ang Sheng, and Chu Te had all died. Teng
was the only Politburo casualty of this period, and his
political demise appeared to further strengthen the
radicals.

The political world now awaited the death of Mao, long
rumored to be suffering from an irreversible malady. On
the surface, politics at the top appeared to be in a state
of suspended animation. In reality, plans were probably
being laid on all sides, with the key struggle being over
the control of Mao--alive and dead. The "April 30th
Directive" is the instrument of Hua and his victorious
coalition in seeking to establish his legitimate succession.
On that date, Hua accompanied New Zealand Prime Minister
Muldoon to see Mao and afterwards remained to report privately on the course of the anti-Teng campaign. Supposedly,
Mao wrote out a three-point directive, the last point of
which was the famous, "With you in charge, I'm at ease."[13]
After the arrest of the Gang of Four, this directive was
widely circulated.

Chiang Ch'ing and her group had their own document,
that of June 3, purporting to represent Mao's instructions
on that date to an assembled group that included most of
the key leaders. According to the radical version, Mao
told them, "In the future, you must help Chiang Ch'ing
carry the red banner and must not let it fall. You must
remind her to avoid making past mistakes."[14] This document,
which the Shanghai Group evidently sought to distribute
widely via stencil after Mao's death, is denounced as a
forgery by the Hua group. They couple this accusation
with a strong denial that Mao wanted his wife to be party
chairman--otherwise, why did he not appoint her first vice-
chairman during his life?

As Mao's end drew near, Chiang Ch'ing and her associates
seem to have maneuvered successfully to control access to
him ever more firmly, with at least one additional member
of the family involved. Mao's nephew, Mao Yuan-hsin,
vice-chairman of the Liaoning Provincial Revolutionary
Committee and secretary of the provincial party, came to
Peking to serve as "liaison officer" during the chairman's
last days, conveying Mao's directives to various departments. A daughter by Chiang Ch'ing, Li Na, may also have
been involved. Both Mao Yuan-hsin and Li Na are reportedly
under arrest as 1976 comes to a close. Certain reports
indicate that Chiang Ch'ing herself had not been living

in the same house as Mao for some time, and there are also
rumors that Mao complained about his unhappy marriage to
close friends--but whatever the facts, Chiang Ch'ing kept
the closest watch over developments as the end approached.

Shortly after Mao died on September 9, she reportedly
went to the General Office of the Central Committee and
took away certain directives of Mao. Later, at the request of Hua, she reportedly returned them, but after "some
tampering." Yet Hua, "seeking unity," is alleged to have
said nothing about the matter at the time. Whatever the
facts, tension clearly rose during the latter part of September. According to one account, Chiang Ch'ing formally proposed to Hua that he support her for the party chairman-
ship. Another report is that she sought to ingratiate herself with Su Chen-hua, deputy commander of the navy, and
indicated to him that the new slate would include Chang
Ch'un-ch'iao as first vice-chairman of the party and premier,
Wang Hung-wen as head of the Military Commission, and Hua
as second vice-chairman. Su supposedly reported this
to Hua.[15]

One must be exceedingly careful of accepting these or
similar stories as the full and unvarnished truth. In the
months and years ahead, we are likely to get many accounts,
varying in considerable measure. Whether we will ever hear
the unexpurgated Shanghai Group version, however, is very
doubtful. In this type of political system, the losers
are never allowed to tell their story to the world first-
hand. It is important, nevertheless, to know what the
victorious team is telling the cadres and the masses.
From these accounts, we can learn much. Whatever the precise truth, it is obvious that China has just witnessed
an extraordinary power struggle replete with extensive
court intrigue and involving all parties at the top of the
political ladder. The critical issue, moreover, was not
any specific substantive question. Rather it was an issue
revealing the very essence of the political system, a
system in which tradition and "Communism" have been intertwined and integrated in remarkable degree. Who is the
legitimate heir--who has the right to inherit Mao's mantle?

Despite the seemingly complete triumph of the veteran
cadres and military men at this point, many questions can
be raised as to the extent to which Mao really belongs
to Hua and his colleagues--and even the extent to which,
privately, they want him. If Mao actually distrusted and
disliked his wife and the Shanghai leaders, why did no
one dare move against them for as long as the chairman
lived? Others, completely dependent upon Mao, like
Ch'en Po-ta, were brought down with the chairman's approval,
but the star of the Shanghai Group steadily rose while
their political opponents were placed always on the defensive. In all probability, Mao did have points of

disagreement and periods of petulance, even anger, with the
Shanghai Group, as with all others who rose high in the
political firmament. No one survived close to Mao easily.
But it cannot be forgotten that Mao was intimately associated with this group for the last decade of his life,
from the onset of the Cultural Revolution, and even before.
The various slogans, symbols, and directives issued in name
or approved by him, moreover, seemed to fit with their views
far better than with those of the moderates.

     Indeed, the least convincing aspect of the current cam-
paign against the Gang of Four is the effort to pin on them
the labels "capitalist-roaders" and "right-wing revisionsists,"
insisting that appellations like "leftist" or "radical" do
not belong to them. The purpose of this effort, of course,
is transparent. Since Mao--and the Chinese Revolution--must
be identified with the left at this stage, the Shanghai
Group must be put in the camp of Liu Shao-ch'i, Lin Piao,
and--ironically--Teng Hsiao-p'ing, who may be at least
partly rehabilitated again. All of this strongly suggests
that the gap between rhetoric and reality will continue in
China, with the rhetoric being "Maoist," namely, hortatory,
highly politicized, and left, while policies betray a
pragmatic, exploratory, complex character.

     Will an overt de-Maoization campaign in the manner of
the Soviet de-Stalinization campaign be launched at some
point, possibly when greater stability prevails? Predictions relating to the long-range future are unwise, but
for the period immediately ahead, such a development seems
unlikely. To attack Mao frontally would be to attack the
entire history of the People's Republic of China, and much
of the history of the Communist Party of China as well. In
Russia, it must be remembered, before Stalin there was Lenin
who is still treated as father of country and of party.
But before Mao?

     The trauma of near-continuous campaigns against once-
revered leaders has already taken a heavy toll. Reports
from travelers coming out of China during the summer of
1976, including overseas Chinese visiting relatives,
indicated a high level of cynicism among lower-ranking
cadres and the people, and a growing laxness in discipline.
The last thing which the PRC needs at this point is another
major political shock. Moreover, it will be recalled
that China has had a lengthy history of being able to
change a dead sage by reinterpreting him. Thus, it seems
probable that Mao will suffer the fate of Confucius, not
Stalin--at least in the immediate future.

     Of at least equal importance is a broader question:
will China be able to achieve political stability at this
point, or do other major upheavals lie ahead? Once again,
this is an issue to be approached with caution and humility.
A number of observers, including specialists, badly

misjudged the recent past--despite an accumulation of
evidence and logic that should have served as warning
signals. The predictions of stability under Teng, then
under Hua as of early 1976 were widespread. But has a
significant corner now been turned, with the ouster of
the Shanghai Group?
     There can be little question, as just noted, that
China desperately needs a period of political calm, a
surcease from the incessant crises that have marked the
past decade. Even this strongly disciplined, highly
organized authoritarian state shows signs of fraying as
a result of too much strain. Despite the bravado expressed
in the Chinese media, moreover, important portions of the
external world are still perceived as hostile or uncertain
in their attitudes toward China, adding to the need for
internal unity. And prolonged political trouble, especially
if it is serious, will adversely affect production in the
future as it has on occasion in the past. Finally, and
most important, the present coalition manning the key posts
at the center seems more compatible than any similar
group since the Cultural Revolution got underway.
     Looking at the other side of the picture, however,
true coalition politics has never been possible in a
modern Communist state, and one must doubt that the PRC
will prove to be an exception. The Communist system demands a pyramidal structure, with one man clearly at the
apex, normally, the secretary-general of the party.
Despite his new titles and the encomiums now being issued
on his behalf, Hua has still to measure up to this challenge. At this point, he is too lacking in lengthy institutional ties or personal connections at the national level
to be independently powerful. The support of men who in
their own right have stronger institutional bases--in
party, administrative organs, and the military branches--
remains indispensable. Hua may acquire the necessary personal power, and surely he will make the effort. But
that in itself will require changes in the status quo,
changes made inevitable in any case by the advanced age
of some of the key actors of the moment.
     Meanwhile, at the provincial levels, some exceedingly
complex and potentially divisive problems exist. Here,
those who gained and those who lost by virtue of the Cultural Revolution currently coexist in various party,
administrative, and military positions, often uneasily,
we may presume. Factional divisions, possibly of lengthy
duration, but in any case exacerbated by the humiliations
and animosities that accompanied the Cultural Revolution,
must be moderated if tranquillity is to prevail. Add to
this the fact that generational differences are becoming
increasingly important, together with the differences
induced from institutional affiliations.

Cognizant that these problems existed in their most immediate acute form in Shanghai following the purge of the Gang of Four, the Hua-Yeh duo moved quickly, both militarily and politically. PLA troops were sent into the city in sufficient number to quell any possible disturbances. At the same time, three top leaders were dispatched to take over the reins of power from the fallen Gang. Su Chen-hua, sixty-seven years of age and rehabilitated after having been purged in 1967, admiral and deputy commander of the navy as well as alternate Politburo member, became first party secretary and head of the municipal Revolutionary Committee. Ni Chih-fu, forty-three years of age and product of the Culrural Revolution--the only counterpart to Wang Hung-wen, being of factory worker background, and recently prominent as a Peking union and militia leader--became second party secretary. Ni is also an alternate member of the Politburo. P'eng Ch'ung, sixty-four years of age and unscathed by the Cultural Revolution, having denounced his superiors and shifted to the left during that period, became third party secretary. P'eng has been a veteran leader in neighboring Kiangsu Province (since 1954), and in addition to his civilian posts, served as political commissar for many years, reaching the rank of lieutenant general. He came from a guerrilla background, probably serving with the New Fourth Army.

The pattern pursued in Shanghai suggests that the effort will continue to mix leaders of different generations, different institutional affiliations, and different career patterns. But this does not guarantee stability, and changes may be necessary in many other provinces. Currently, there are reports of trouble in Fukien, and indeed, the rapid turnover of provincial secretaries in various of the provinces in South China in recent years suggests unresolved conflicts in many places. Provincial allegiance to center directives also has varied, possibly because provincial leaders knew of the divisions in Peking. Rank disobedience is virtually impossible to find, but procrastination and the construction of Potemkin villages serve as passable substitutes.

On the plus side, satisfactory to good production records in recent years, both in agriculture and in industry, have aided in keeping dissidence down. At the mass levels in China, the most volatile conditions are likely to ensue from economic rather than political grievances. Yet there are economic issues of great consequence that require decisions, and some could lead to further political problems. For example, shall factory wages continue to be frozen, at the risk of further trouble such as that which erupted in Hangchow and some other industrial centers? What of the "down to the countryside" movement, and commune policies in general?

Given the overall balance sheet, it seems logical to
assume that for the near future, major political upheavals
have a lower probability than in the last ten years. To
make this statement, however, one must set aside the possibility of some major unforeseeable event such as war,
assassination, or drastic economic reverses. And even if
the immediate future is one of greater domestic tranquillity,
China is likely to suffer recurrent political instability
over the middle and long-range future. The first-generation
leaders are almost gone at this point, but a clear hierarchy
among the succeeding groups has not been established, nor
will it come easily. The fissures that flow from the Cultural Revolution--and in a more fundamental sense, both
from Chinese political culture and from Communism--will not
disappear, and they affect civil and military ranks alike.
In sum, Mao has left behind him weak institutions and powerful personalities, a combination prone to unexpected changes
and periodic upheavals.

Given the situation, any political leader in China who
forgets one of Mao's favorite maxims, "Political power grows
out of the barrel of a gun," is likely to have a short tenure.
Thus, even if the top leader is a civilian, the military are
almost certain to play a critical role in future, as they
have in the past. In one sense, this symbolizes the fact
that for China, the nation-building process is far from
complete. Despite the enormous emphasis upon nationalism
in recent decades, regional differences persist, as do
ethnic ones. South China, in particular, has its own sub-
culture, but so do other regions. Ethnic minorities are
scarcely 8 percent of the total population, but they are
largely concentrated in China's sensitive border regions.
It is not surprising that in most of these border provinces,
top political power has consistently been held by professional military men in recent years, irrespective of the
precise hierarchy in Peking.

Is there a possibility that China might disintegrate
into chaos and civil war? Nothing is impossible in the politics of our times, but the breakup of China does not seem
likely. In addition to the strong nationalist thrust of
recent decades, transport and communications improvements
now make possible a rapid movement of military forces when
trouble is threatened. Only a sustained, serious breach
in the topmost political-military ranks in Peking would constitute a serious threat in this direction, and while this
cannot be totally ruled out given the events of the recent
past, survival up to date suggests continued viability.

Thus, it is appropriate at this point to turn from the
politics of personalities, factions, and institutions to
those of issues, acknowledging once again their interrela-
tion. What substantive issues are likely to command the
Chinese future, and what clues do we currently have as to

their resolutions? Many tough decisions will have to be
made in the economic category, as has been emphasized.
Before exploring these, let us provide a brief tour d'
horizon of the economic situation in its broadest dimen-
sions.16

   Recent studies suggest that industrial production in
China has risen on an average of 9 percent in the decade
beginning in 1965, with producer goods output growing as
much as 14 percent per annum, on an average; industrial
consumer goods, 7 percent, or one-half that amount. Agricultural production has also risen, but naturally by a much
smaller amount, possibly by 3 percent per annum average, or
somewhat less. Some authorities, indeed, believe that agricultural gains have barely kept pace with population increases, which are estimated to have been 2.3 percent in
1970, dropping to 1.8 percent in 1975. Taking all factors
into account, China's overall gross national product has
probably averaged a growth of about 5 percent per annum over
the past two decades.17

   Given the magnitude of the problems, the mistakes made,
and the sporadic political upheavals characterizing these
years, that is an impressive record. Students may debate
how to divide the credit between Chinese culture and governmental policies. In any case, however, important decisions lie ahead, albeit decisions limited by some stern
realities. There seems little doubt that agriculture must
remain "the foundation" of China's economic modernization,
granting industry the role of "leading factor." But can
agriculture production be stimulated sufficiently to keep
the pace of growth at a satisfactory level? Major gains
in water conservancy and irrigation, especially in the
rice-growing areas, were the first step, enabling a lessened
dependence upon weather conditions, and the expansion of
double and triple cropping together with increases in
arable acreages. Advances in scientific agriculture
followed, with advantage being taken of gains in technology abroad. And in the past decade, gains have been
increasingly due to the increased use of chemical fertilizer. Perhaps the easier tasks have been largely accom-
plished, however. Ahead lies the need for very large-
scale water conservancy programs and massive reforestation
in the north. Mechanization on a greatly augmented scale
will also be essential at some point. But the costs of
these and similar programs are very high.

   Can a further reduction of population increases take
place? Here, the Chinese have apparently achieved very
considerable success, although rural resistance may have
been greater than is acknowledged. Almost surely, the
campaign will continue, even be accelerated. Can the rate
of investment in agriculture and in agricultural-related
industries be raised? This will not be easy, given what

are going to be heightened consumer pressures for more food
and clothing. Gains thus far have been attained at the
price of postponing consumer benefits in substantial measure. A very sizable portion of the peasantry still live
close to the marginal levels of subsistence. And the
unrest among urban workers in recent years has given rise
to concern, even the need for military intervention in
select areas. Moreover, the pressures for increased military expenditures may well be the price to be paid for the
indispensable support of the key military leaders.

To what extent can the problem be alleviated by a
turning outward, a borrowing or purchasing of technology
from abroad? The theme of self-reliance, so powerfully
directed toward the Third World as well as toward the
Chinese people, will certainly not be abandoned. Here,
Chinese tradition and Maoist ideology combine to sustain
a set of mind, a bent toward principle--even at a cost.
In addition, some practical obstacles are posed, chief
among them the question of foreign exchange. The much-
vaunted oil deposits, while important, may not prove to
be the complete answer as predicted by some enthusiasts.
In the final analysis, however, one might anticipate that
China will be drawn into a more involved, complex economic
relation with the advanced, industrial world. The questions relate primarily to timing and degree.

Meanwhile, the issue of economic incentives will
stubbornly refuse to disappear. Up to date, Chinese policies have generally prevented the urban-rural gap from
growing wider, and indeed, that gap may have been reduced,
as the leadership claims. Urbanites, however, have higher
living standards on the average, and by a considerable
measure. Moreover, at both levels, the worker and his
family are certain to push for improvements. The bicycle
culture moves forward, as does that of the radio--not to
mention the importance of such items as food and clothing.
Whatever the rhetoric, therefore, it is likely that the
present incentive structure will remain, and quite possibly
it will be necessary to make labor more attractive in monetary terms, particularly for the urban worker. The private
plots will also continue to be a vital part of the Chinese
economy. But the commune system, including its small and
medium industrial components, will probably survive.

Issues relating to industrial management and the locus
of decision making will also continue to be in the forefront of discussion. In all probability, experimentation
backward and forward will take place, with both ideological and practical considerations hovering over the action.
Revolution and development will both present their claims.
In the long term, development is almost certain to win,
although the pattern may be a zigzag one. And development
is likely to mean tighter managerial controls, greater

centralization, and increased bureaucratization at every
level. Periodically, these trends will be challenged, but
they will also be defended on the usual grounds: the need
to allocate raw materials and manpower efficiently, improving the quality of production, and making decisions with
security factors and sectoral advantages taken into consideration. Naturally, none of these issues will ever be
finally settled.

Higher education and cultural concerns will also
receive close attention, and some changes are probable.
Once again, this does not mean that the old rhetoric will
be completely abandoned. The Cultural Revolution will continue to be defended. Even revolutionary opera may survive
despite the demise of its leading proponent. Certainly,
the principle of opening higher education to "workers,
peasants, and soldiers" will be sustained, and many of the
new vocational schools now labeled colleges and universities will continue. But at the major institutions of
higher learning some renewed commitment to quality will
ultimately be made, even if this is done softly and in
stages.

While the debate over educational policies has been a
public, angry affair, that over military policies has
understandably been conducted in the strictest privacy.
We cannot know, therefore, the precise issues or divisions
of recent times but drawing upon some earlier data, we can
at least attempt educated guesses.

If the major threat is presumed to come from the
Soviet Union, it is difficult to fault the general strategy
usually ascribed to Mao of relying heavily upon the mobilized
masses for a defense in depth. In truth, no other defense
could readily be constructed. But in the aftermath of the
costly Korean War, Chinese military leaders got a taste of
modernization with Soviet support. From this point on,
the question of "professionalization," namely, an emphasis
upon both weaponry and military training, relegating
political and economic chores to a distinctly secondary
position, was pushed to the forefront.

In one sense, this was yet another branch of the "Red"
versus "expert" controversy. Yet it went considerably
beyond this. Amidst the competitive bid for state investment, how should the military be ranked in comparison with
industry at any given point? Until a firm industrial base
had been constructed, the military along with all other
elements making up the Chinese state would be at a signal
disadvantage. Further, there was the complex issue of the
relative priority to give the nuclear program versus conventional weapons.

While the course of debate/consensus over these issues
is cloaked in considerably mystery, differences are apparent via the changes in personnel and policies that have

occurred. In general, it would appear that for a combination of reasons, the militia program was accelerated in
the post-Cultural Revolution period, and the nuclear
program was also given top priority--albeit, not without
some problems being encountered. The record with respect
to the conventional armed forces is less positive. Most
sources indicate that China's conventional weaponry is anti-
quated, and in recent years it would appear that expenditures in this area have generally contracted rather than
expanded, possibly in part to enable a careful study of
the directions to be taken and the external sources to be
utilized.

What lies ahead? The PRC at this point gives every
indication of intending to push its nuclear program strongly.
The hope that China wll negotiate controls or limits on its
nuclear weapons at this stage are faint indeed, as is
illustrated by Peking's present demand for "a total ban on
nuclear weapons" as the only acceptable approach--knowing
full well that this is a complete nonstarter. It seems
likely that while the Chinese leaders know that they cannot hope to compete in this field with either the United
States or the USSR, they are resolved to have--at a minimum--
a "credible deterrent," presumably a second strike capacity.

One may expect, however, that there will also be an
increased effort to upgrade conventional military weapons,
especially in terms of air and sea power, and a renewed
emphasis upon professionalism throughout the armed services. The militia is not likely to be abandoned, but one
can guess that its leadership will not be allowed to oper-
ate independently and in a competitive fashion with the
PLA, as was recently threatened. And whatever the basic
budgetary decisions, the military is probably going to have
a strong voice in the near future at least. There are few
if any interest groups in a better political position at
present, assuming internal unity can be achieved.

The above issues cannot be separated from foreign
policy concerns, and the truly critical issues in foreign
policy today pertain to Sino-Soviet relations. Neither war
nor alliance between the two Communist giants seems likely.
War could not conceivably benefit either side. Alliance
seems totally unfeasible, given the range of differences
that now prevail. The choice is a more narrow one, yet
one of very great importance. Should a conscious effort
be made to reduce tension, with some improvements in
state-to-state relations sought, or is it to be continued
hostility short of conflict?

The advantages of the former course would appear to
be considerable for the Chinese. By reducing tension,
the risks of confrontation would be lessened and, possibly, some of the urgency for greatly increasing military
expenditures. In general, moreover, Chinese foreign policy

could enjoy greater flexibility, with the possibility of
Peking's being able to play Washington off against Moscow.
    On the other hand, there are clear advantages at this
critical juncture in Chinese politics in having an external
enemy, a rallying point in promoting unity and sacrifice.
The United States can no longer play that role effectively,
given recent developments. More importantly, the deep
hatred of the Russians in many Chinese circles is difficult
to exaggerate, and it is matched by the widest conceivable
range of differences over ideological and substantive
issues.
    Up to late 1976, the attack upon the Soviet government
in the official Chinese press remained as severe as it had
been previously. The "Brezhnev clique" continued to be
described as "revisionsists, social imperialists and
Fascists"--"a gang that had led their country out of the
socialist camp back to capitalism." There are few epithets
that remain unused, and from some of them, it will be
difficult to back away. Yet the border talks have resumed
once again, and given the eagerness of the Russians to
improve relations, the initiative lies with Peking. Whatever the decisions, they will have far-reaching consequences.
    Some of the repercussions relate to Sino-American rela-
tions. In recent times, Chinese foreign policy has rested
upon balance-of-power principles. The world has been
divided into three parts: the two superpowers, the Second
Intermediate Zone (Japan and Western Europe), and the Third
World. The task is to build a united front against the
primary enemy, the Soviet Union. This involves a limited
detente with the other superpower, the United States;
closer relations with the advanced capitalist nations; and
the closest possible identificaton with the Third World.
This basic policy has been derived from the Communist
strategy within China after the onset of the Sino-Japanese
War in 1937. Then Japan was the primary enemy, necessitat-
ing an alliance with the Kuomintang, a cultivation of the
"national bourgeoisie," together with an effort to lead the
Chinese peasants and workers.
    Thus, the relationship with the United States has been
a tactical one, in no sense based on ideological or political convergence. Nor has it precluded rigorous criticism.
At the same time, however, the main concern expressed by
Chinese leaders since the Indochina debacle has been
whether the American will and commitment are such as to
withstand Soviet pressures. Frequently, the specter of
Munich and the dangers of appeasement are raised in the
Chinese media. The PRC has not wanted the United States
to be present everywhere in Asia, but it has clearly
wanted American power in some areas to offset a growing
Soviet presence throughout the region. And there have
been no more ardent supporters of NATO and a unified

Western Europe than the spokesmen for Peking.

While supporting Western unity and urging a firm response to Russian "social imperialism," the Chinese leaders have also offered a prediction: World War III is inevitable, and it will be a confrontation between the Americans and Russians centering upon Europe. Is the wish father to the thought? An ancient Chinese proverb speaks of sitting on the mountaintop, watching two tigers fight.

In the long run--or perhaps more accurately, in the shortest possible time--China intends to be a major power, and recognized as such. In this connection, if its goals are reached, it will first be a major power in Asia. And despite its ardent insistence that it will never seek hegemony anywhere, China's nationalism cum Communism is likely to bear down heavily on most if not all Asian states, whatever their political coloration of the moment. This fact alone suggests that the future path of Sino-Soviet relations is not likely to be a smooth one, whatever the tactical twists and turns of any given period. For Russia too intends to be a major power--on a global scale--and recognized as such. In the coming decades, moreover, Russian power--military and economic--will almost surely grow in the "far eastern" portions of the Soviet Union, making Russia a rising Asian power. Given the uneasy situation that exists in the Central Asian interior, on both sides of the Sino-Soviet border, and the absence of any buffer state system such as abetted European detente, the task of adjusting Sino-Soviet relations will be the more difficult.

If the course of Sino-Soviet relations is likely to be complex and troubled, there is little reason to believe that China's leaders will commit themselves to an alliance with the United States. Here, too, relations are destined to be complex, with elements of cooperation (or acquies- cence) and conflict both involved. Nor does Japan seem a likely ally in the traditional sense. Only an imminent threat of conflict with the USSR could drive China to seek something approximating alliance. The PRC will continue to play upon the themes of independence and self-reliance, with an ample quotient of xenophobia present--while slowly entering into a network of new relations with the external world. The tempo and directon of these relations will be largely dependent upon three variables: the prevailing balance of internal political forces; the perception of the external threat; and the evolution of international politics, or what is sometimes called the "international order."

One final word would seem in order. In the recent past, American writing--including professional writing-- on contemporary China has moved from simplicity to

complexity, romanticism to realism, with an admixture of
humility. These trends are in the right direction. No
one can predict the precise Chinese leaders or policies of
the future. At best, the more credible alternatives can
be discerned, and some probabilities advanced. But can
we do much more with respect to our own society in this
troubled, transitional era?

NOTES

1. Jen-min Jih-pao [People's Daily], Nov. 1, 1976, p. 1.
2. A number of general works covering the history of
the Communist movement have now been published, with varying perspectives involved. Among those which I have recom-
mended are: Lucien Bianco, Origins of the Chinese Revolu-
tion--1915-1949 (Stanford: Stanford Univ. Press, 1971);
C. P. FitzGerald, The Birth of Communist China (rev. ed.,
New York: Praeger, 1964); Jacques Guillermaz, Histoire du
parti communiste Chinois (Paris, 1967); James Pinckney
Harrison, The Long March to Power--A History of the Chinese
Communist Party, 1921-72 (New York: Praeger, 1972); Franklin
W. Houn, A Short History of Chinese Communism (rev. ed.,
Englewood Cliffs, N.J.: Prentice-Hall, 1973); and Warren
Kuo, Analytical History of the Chinese Community Party, vols.
1-4, (Taipei: Institute of International Relations, 1968).
3. For an interesting collection of documents per-
taining to the Peng purge, see The Case of Peng Teh-huai--
1959-1968 (Hong Kong: Union Research Institute, 1968).
4. A rich variety of articles on the Chinese commune
system are to be found in Asian Survey, China Quarterly,
and the Far Eastern Economic Review. An early Communist
perspective is presented in Hsueh Mu-chiao, Su Hsing, and
Lin Tse-li, The Socialist Transformation of the National
Economy in China (Peking: Foreign Languages Press); see
also, C. S. Chen and Charles P. Ridley, ed. and trans.,
Rural People's Communes in Lien-chiang (Stanford: Hoover
Institution Press, 1969); Richard Baum, Prelude to Revolu-
tion--Mao, the Party, and the Peasant Question, 1962-66
(New York: Columbia Univ. Press, 1975); Kenneth R. Walker,
Planning in Chinese Agriculture--Socialization and the
Private Sector, 1956-62 (Chicago: Aldine, 1965); and
Richard Hughes, The Chinese Communes (London: Bodley, 1960).
5. See Theodore H. E. Chen, Thought Reform of the
Chinese Intellectuals (Hong Kong: Hong Kong Univ. Press,
1960); David Kan, The Impact of the Cultural Revolution
on Chinese Higher Education (Hong Kong: Union Research
Institute, 1970); Roderick MacFarquhar, The Origins of
the Cultural Revolution (New York: Columbia Univ. Press,
1964); R. F. Price, Education in Communist China (New
York: Praeger, 1970); and Peter J. Seybolt, Revolutionary

Education in China--Documents and Commentary (White Plains,
N.Y.: International Arts and Sciences Press, 1973).
    6. See Robert A. Scalapino, "The Struggle over Higher
Education--Revolution versus Development," Issues and Studies
12, no. 7 (July 1976): 1-8.
    7. In addition to the important articles appearing in
Asian Survey and China Quarterly, see Chien Yu-Shen, China's
Fading Revolution--Army Dissent and Military Divisions,
1967-68 (Hong Kong: Centre of Contemporary Chinese Studies,
1969); Angus M. Fraser, The People's Liberation Army--
Communist China's Armed Forces (New York: Crane, Russak
and Co., 1973); John Gittings, The Role of the Chinese
Army (London: Oxford Univ. Press, 1967); Samuel B. Griffith
II, The Chinese People's Liberation Army (New York, McGraw-
Hill, 1967); Harry Harding and Melvin Gurtov, The Purge of
Lo Jui-ching: The Politics of Chinese Strategic Planning
(Santa Monica: Rand, 1970); Ellis Joffe, Party and Army:
Professionalism and Political Control in the Chinese Officer
Corps, 1949-1964 (Cambridge, Mass.: Harvard Univ. Press,
1965); William Whitson, ed., The Military and Political
Power in China in the 1970s (New York: Praeger, 1972);
Selected Military Writings of Mao Tse-tung (Peking:
Foreign Languages Press, 1968).
    8. Robert A. Scalapino, "The CCPs Provincial Secre-
taries," Problems of Communism, July-August 1976, pp.
18-35.
    9. See Scalapino, "The Transition in Chinese Party
Leadership: A Comparison of the Eighth and Ninth Central
Committees," in Robert A. Scalapino, ed., Elites in the
People's Republic of China, (Seattle: Univ. of Washington
Press, 1972).
    10. See Tai Sung An, The Lin Piao Affair, Research
Monograph no. 17 (Philadelphia: Foreign Policy Research
Institute, 1974).
    11. For three general works on politics of this era
of great interest, see A. Doak Barnett, Uncertain Passage
(Washington, D.C.: The Brookings Institution, 1974);
Parris H. Chang, Power and Policy in China (University
Park: Pennsylvania State Univ. Press, 1975); and Jurgen
Domes, The Internal Politics of China, 1949-1972 (New York:
Praeger, 1973).
    Significant studies of Mao recently published include
Robert J. Lifton, Revolutionary Immortality--Mao Tse-tung
and the Chinese Cultural Revolution (revised ed., New
York: W. W. Norton, 1968); Lucian W. Pye, Mao Tse-tung,
The Man in the Leader (New York: Basic Books, 1976);
Edward E. Rice, Mao's Way (Berkeley: Univ. of California
Press, 1972); and Richard H. Solomon, Mao's Revolution
and the Chinese Political Culture (Berkeley: Univ. of
California Press, 1971).
    12. Scalapino, "The CCPs Provincial Secretaries," p. 27.

13.   See the speech of Wu Teh of Oct. 24, 1976,
reproduced in Ta-kung Pao [L'Impartial], Oct. 28, 1976,
pp. 3.
14.   For example, see the account published in Ming
Pao (Hong Kong), Oct. 29, 1976, of the reports by Hua
Kuo-feng, Yeh Chien-ying, and Wang Tung-hsing at a meeting
of the Politburo on the crisis on Oct. 7, and carried in
Foreign Broadcast Information Service (FBIS), Daily Report:
People's Republic of China, Nov. 1, 1976, p. E2-4.
15.   FBIS, Daily Report: People's Republic of China,
Nov. 1, 1976, E4.
16.   For three relatively recent works of importance
on the general economic picture, see People's Republic of
China: An Economic Assessment, Joint Economic Committee,
U. S. Congress (Washington, D.C.:   U.S. Government Printing
Office, 1972); Bryant G. Garth and the Editors of the
Stanford Journal of International Studies, China's Changing
Role in the World Economy, (New York: Praeger, 1975); and
Allocation of Resources in the Soviet Union and China--
1976, Hearings before the Subcommittee on Priorities and
Economy in Government, Joint Economic Committee, U.S.
Congress, May 24 and June 15, 1976.
17.   See Dwight H. Perkins, "The Constraints on
Chinese Foreign Policy," in Donald C. Hellmann, ed.,
China and Japan: A New Balance of Power (Lexington,
Mass.: Lexington Books, 1976). Perkins makes the point
that the difference between a possible 5% average GNP
growth and one of 7% in the period ahead would have far-
reaching implications for both China and the world; but
he does not venture a hard prediction as to which he
thinks is more probable.

2. The Chinese Economy in the 1970s: Performances, Problems, and Prospects

Nai-ruenn Chen

Introduction

A number of momentous events took place in China in 1976. The death of Chou En-lai in January led to an acceleration of the antirightist campaign in the spring and the Tien-an-men incident in April, resulting in the dismissal of Teng Hsiao-p'ing and the rise of Hua Kuo-feng to the premiership. The earthquake in July, which caused devastating damages to the economy and population in the Tangshan and Tientsin area, was followed by the death of Mao Tse-tung in September. Within a month of the passing of Mao, his widow and her political associates in the Politburo who had held second, fourth, and fifth places in the party were purged, and Premier Hua became chairman of the Communist Party of China. Toward the end of 1976 there had been an intensified campaign against the followers of the four discredited leaders throughout the country and a tighter military control of some provinces.

Any one of these events would have certain impact, directly or indirectly, on the Chinese economy; their combined effect, therefore, must be significant. In fact, problems and uncertainties permeate nearly all sectors of the Chinese economy. National output in 1976, however, appears to have continued to grow, albeit only moderately. This is partly because efforts were made to keep the disruptive effects of the various events at a minimum, and partly because the growth momentum which the economy built up in the first half of the 1970s continued in 1976. The rate and pattern of China's economic growth in the remainder of the 1970s depends on the course which the new leadership will take in directing, planning, and managing the economy.

This chapter attempts to assess the Chinese economy in the 1970s from the vantage point of late 1976. After a review of China's economic policies, the chapter discusses the performance and problems of major economic sectors, some population and labor issues of critical importance to China's economic development, and the prospects for future growth.

Economic Policy and Planning

A primary economic goal of the People's Republic of China is to build the country into a modern economic power under socialism and with a high degree of autarky. To attain the goal a two-stage developmental program, reportedly originated by Mao, was outlined by the late

Chou En-lai in a report to the National People's Congress
in January 1975. The first stage is to build what Chou
called "an independent and relatively comprehensive industrial and economic system" before 1980; the second stage
is to accomplish "the comprehensive modernization of agriculture, industry, national defense and science and technology" so that China will become an advanced country before
the end of the century.

The developmental program was vigorously pursued by
Chou, and later by Teng. During the antirightist campaign
in the spring and summer of 1976, Teng's measures to implement the program, particularly those related to technology
imports, raw material exports, the expansion of labor-
intensive export industries, material incentives, and
industrial management, came under heavy ideological attack
from his political opponents. For months there were
hesitations and uncertainties among China's policymakers
as to what course they should take in moving the Chinese
economy. After the purge of the "radical" members from
the Chinese leadership in October, China will probably
continue to adopt Chou-Teng economic policies directed
toward achievement of the year 2000 objectives. In fact,
these objectives were emphatically restated in a joint
editorial after Hua's appointment to the party chairman-
ship,[1] and in a subsequent series of other official pro-
nouncements.

The attainment of these objectives depends critically
on the ability of the Chinese to develop a viable agricultural sector. China still is a predominantly agricultural
country with 80 percent of the population living in the
rural areas. Any modernization program requires the peasants to produce an adequate surplus of food and fibers
over and above their own consumption to support labor
engaged in nonagricultural activities and provide raw
materials for industrial production and exports. Without
a growing agricultural base, overall economic growth
would be difficult to sustain over prolonged periods.
The Chinese became fully aware of this as a result of their
policy experiments in the First Five-Year Plan (FYP)
(1953-57) and Great Leap Forward (1958-59). During these
periods their policy of concentrating investment in industry combined with rapid population growth resulted in the
failure of agriculture to expand surpluses for the support of industrialization. In the early 1960s a complete
reversal in planning priorities evolved, with agriculture
first, followed by light industry and heavy industry, in
turn. This order of planning priorities has remained
intact to this day.

A renewed emphasis on agricultural development has
been noted in the past year following a national conference
at Tachai in Shansi Province. Several thousand persons,

including a number of top leaders, participated in the
conference, convened by the State Council in September
1975. The major goals for agricultural development were
outlined in a keynote speech delivered by the then Deputy
Premier Hua Kuo-feng. The conference called for each
county in China to "completely carry out the national
economic policy of taking agriculture as the foundation
and industry as the leading factor" by raising agricultural
productivity more rapidly with emphasis on the expansion of
farm capital construction and farm mechanization. These
goals were stressed once again by Hua at the second
national agricultural conference held in December 1976.
     Assigning agriculture the highest priority does not
imply that a major portion of investable resources are
allocated to agriculture, but rather ensures an adequate
supply of capital and material inputs to meet the required
rate of agricultural growth. State investment in agriculture has been stepped up, and industries producing
inputs for agricultural production have been greatly expanded. According to a preliminary estimate, since the
early 1960s resources approximating 10 billion yuan (or
roughly U.S. $5 billion) a year have been invested in
agriculture and supporting industries in addition to what
would have been invested had the agriculture-first policy
not been introduced.[2] Although investment in agriculture
increased significantly in both absolute level and relative share, the bulk of state resources still went to
industry and modern transport.
     Relative investment priorities within each sector of
the economy are subject to shifts and are usually set in
annual and five-year plans. Since 1960 the Chinese have
made it a practice not to publish any detail of their
economic plans. The current Five-Year Plan, the original
blueprint of which was masterminded by Teng Hsiao-p'ing
and his advisors, was due to have commenced in January
1976, but was delayed by the anti-Teng campaign earlier
in the year. Official sources have indicated that the
plan is now under revision and will probably be formally
adopted in 1977.

Agricultural Production

In spite of the official policy of according agriculture
the first place in planning priority, China's agricultural
production during 1970-75 grew only at an average rate of
2 percent per year, representing virtually no improvement
over the past performance. Grain production in the same
period increased at an average annual rate of less than 2
percent, hardly keeping in pace with population growth.
Output in 1975, estimated at 260 million tons, was at the
same level attained in 1974.[3] The output of cotton,

China's most important industrial crop, has fluctuated
between the annual levels of 2 to 2.5 million tons since
1970. The estimated output of 2.3 million tons in 1975
failed to surpass the record cotton level of 2.5 million
tons in 1973-74. Adverse weather conditions in 1976 led to
very little improvement in Chinese agricultural production.
The preliminary assessment is for outputs in 1976 similar
in size to those of 1975, but in the interim the population
grew by approximately 15 million people.

If Chinese agriculture is to generate a growing surplus to support industrialization, it will have to increase
its output substantially above the 1970-76 level. This
will be a formidable task. Indeed, it would be a remarkable
achievement if China could increase grain production over
3 percent annually in the next few years. Any estimate of
China's grain production at a level beyond 300 million tons
for 1980 is considered too optimistic.

Many factors make the growth of China's agricultural
production difficult. First of all is the scarcity of
cultivable land. Since the greater proportion of cultivable
land in China had long been occupied and tilled, any
remaining area could be opened up only with a considerable
amount of capital investment. The present level of cultivated acreage is probably not much higher than the
1956-57 level. The PRC appears to have resorted to multiple
cropping, a traditional Chinese method for intensive exploitation of land, to expand crop acreage.[4] However, the bulk
of the gains from this technique may have been realized;
multiple cropping has already been extensively practiced
in the south and central rice-growing region, and is
difficult to pursue in most of north China due to a short
growing season or inadequate water supplies.[5]

With the limited supply of land, output can be raised
by the increased use of fertilizers, particularly chemical
fertilizers. Domestic production of chemical fertilizers
has risen rapidly, particularly since the adoption of the
agriculture-first policy in the early 1960s, reaching
27,875 thousand tons in 1975, of which nearly 17 million
tons were produced by rural small-scale plants. Imports
averaged annually 7.5 million tons during 1970-73, but
declined to over 5 million tons in both 1974 and 1975 as a
result of rapidly rising prices in the international
fertilizer market and China's foreign exchange problems.
By 1975 chemical fertilizer use had risen from 4 to 5
kilograms (of nutrients) per hectare of cultivated land
in the mid-1950s to approximately 70 kilograms per hectare
(kg/ha), a level slightly above the world average but
well below the rate attained in Japan and some other
East Asian countries.[6]

If the total nutrients from organic sources are
included, the overall level of fertilizer application
in 1975 at a minimum may be put at 125 kg/ha.[7] Since

about two-thirds of China's farmland is under multiple
cropping, the average amount of fertilizers, both chemical and traditional, applied to each unit of sown area
is probably still lower than the world average. There
still appears to be ample opportunity for China to raise
unit yields by increased use of fertilizer.

     Since 1973 China has purchased thirteen large am-
monia-urea fertilizer complexes which, when completed,
will produce some 18 million tons of nitrogent annually.
If together both modern and rural small-scale plants
produce 70 million tons of fertilizer in 1980 (average
nutrient value 20 percent), then the level of chemical
fertilizer application would reach 125 kg/ha, nearly
doubling 1975 levels. Total fertilizer use, including
organics, could amount to over 200 kg/ha.

     How much would such a fairly large increase in fertil-
izer application contribute to crop production? Available
evidence seems to suggest that the stage of diminishing
returns in fertilizer application in China had already set
in by the late 1960s largely because the use of certain
complementary inputs did not increase fast enough. All
other factors being held constant, the marginal yield
response to fertilizers is bound to decline, perhaps
rapidly, in the future. To raise crop yields, an increasing fertilization must be accompanied by a corresponding
increase in the use of complementary inputs, particularly
water and fertilizer-responsive plant varieties.

     Water control has always been given a high priority
in China's program for agricultural development. The
main measures adopted in recent years have been to bring
sufficient and timely supplies of water to the dry lands,
especially those in the north. The cultivated area under
irrigation expanded from approximately 40 million hectares
in 1970 to about 47 million hectares in 1975. Most of
the 7-million-hectare increase was made possible by the
intensified effort to develop all types of wells; especially important were power-pump wells. They numbered
600,000 in 1971 and reached about 2 million in 1975, of
which 1.7 million were located in North China, particularly Honan and Hopei provinces.

     The total irrigated acreage in China will probably
continue to expand, but at reduced rates. In the southern
and central rice-growing regions, where irrigation facilities began to be built 1,000 years ago, the potential for
additional irrigated acreage appears limited. Neither
can irrigated areas in much of the north be extended much
farther because part of the farmland in the northern provinces, which could be effectively irrigated by wells,
has now been generally brought under irrigation.[8]

     The process of developing fertilizer-responsive
plant varieties is also slow. The prospect of importing

these varieties from abroad does not appear promising,
largely because most of them may not be adaptable to
Chinese conditions and because the present level of
Chinese scientific capability is not sufficient to effect
modifications. Thus new and more fertilizer-responsive
seeds will have to be developed in China.

The Chinese apply the mass line approach to agricultural research by scattering agricultural scientists
throughout the countryside "to learn from the peasant
masses at the grassroots level." In 1975 over 13 million
"farmer scientists and technicians" worked to breed, pro-
pagate, spread, purify, and regenerate fine seed strains.
Such progress, however, has generally been confined within
local areas without a high degree of scientific sophisti-
cation. Whether the Chinese approach will achieve the
badly needed technological breakthroughs in seed development is doubtful. In the opinion of the American Plant
Studies Delegation that visited China in 1974, the level
of Chinese genetic research is about twenty-five years
behind that of the West.

In recent years, considerable efforts have been made
to expand the use of farm machinery and equipment; output
has grown at a rate of more than 10 percent a year. Particular attention has been given to powered irrigation and
drainage equipment for pumping water from wells, for raising water to high lying fields, and for draining water-
logged farmland.[9] The rationale behind the Chinese decision
to expand the use of irrigation and drainage equipment
seems to be partly based on land-saving considerations,
since traditional methods of irrigation may require larger
areas of land than the use of mechanical power. But the
available information does not indicate any significant
expansion of cultivated acreage in China in recent years.

Much of the new farm machinery introduced since 1970
has been to improve labor efficiency, ease pressure on
labor demand in peak seasons, or facilitate the development
of intensive cropping patterns. For example, one of
China's major agricultural mechanization targets has been
the development of mechanical rice transplanters since a
chief obstacle to the efficient operation of double
cropping is the time-consuming process of transplanting
rice seedlings. Although the introduction of such new
machines may improve crop yields directly, the main effect
is to reduce the work burden on farmers. A more important
objective of the current drive to mechanize agriculture
is to seek a solution over the larger run of releasing
more rural labor for nonagricultural activities. With
the rapid growth of industry, China is gradually moving
toward the stage where the demand for industrial labor
cannot be sufficiently met without seriously affecting
agricultural production.

All in all, one should not expect major breakthroughs
in Chinese agricultural production in the next few years.
To ensure a continuation of agricultural growth, China
will have to continue to commit a large portion of its
resources to agriculture. Unless weather conditions
improve substantially in the years to come, the process
of growth will be, like what has been in the past, unspec-
tacular and painfully slow.

Industrial Development

The rate and pattern of China's industrial growth has been
affected by the magnitude and priority given industrial
investment. It is doubtful whether recent allocations of
state investment in industry have approached the relative
share achieved in the forced march to industrialization in
the 1950s, although absolute levels have increased and in
the early 1970s were higher than in the 1950s or the
1960s.[10] But there has been a rapid growth of rural industry since 1970, developed primarily with local investment, which in the early 1970s was undoubtedly considerably
larger than in the 1950s and the 1960s. The allocative
pattern of total industrial investment in recent years has
greatly affected the sectoral, regional, and rural-urban
distribution of Chinese industry.
      Industrial production grew on the average 10 percent a
year between 1970 and 1975.[11] Considerable surplus capacity
in 1969 at the end of the Cultural Revolution permitted
industrial output to move up rapidly in 1970 at a rate of
19 percent. When output approached capacity, industrial
growth settled to the lower and yet still respectable rates
of 9 percent a year in 1971 and 1972 and 12 percent in
1973, but dropped to 4 percent in 1974. The difficulties
in 1974 probably stemmed partly from disruptions in factories and mines caused by labor unrest, and partly from
the heavy emphasis of investment in the post-Cultural
Revolution years on a few industries such as chemical
fertilizers and petroleum to the neglect of some others
such as the mining sector. The poor performance in mining
appeared to hold back the steel and coal industries. Although bottlenecks still persisted in major industries
in the following year, the easing of factional wrangling
may have contributed to the 10 percent increase in industrial production in 1975. Official statistics indicate
that industrial output grew 7 percent in the first half
of 1976.[12] The devastating earthquakes that struck Hopei
Province in July and Szechwan Province in August and the
continuing campaign against the moderate economic policy
during July through September must have an adverse effect
on industrial growth in the third quarter of 1976.[13] The
rate of industrial growth for 1976 is preliminarily

estimated at 5 percent.

In the period 1970-76, as in previous periods, output of producer goods tended to grow faster than that of consumer goods. Among producer goods, the output of crude oil, chemical fertilizers, and certain agricultural machines including powered irrigation equipment and tractors grew most rapidly. On the other hand, the rates of increase in the output of steel, coal, cement, timber, and machine tools appeared to fall below the average. The output of cotton cloth, China's most important manufactured consumer product, has experienced very little growth since 1970.

The spatial distribution of Chinese industry continued to undergo gradual shifts. Generally speaking, industrially backward provinces, which are mostly in the interior, tend to develop more rapidly than more advanced provinces, most of which are located in the coastal areas. This is the result of China's investment policy favoring backward, interior regions. Kwangsi Chuang and Tibet autonomous regions and all northwestern provinces grew most rapidly. Although heavy investment in these backward provinces led to high growth rates, simply because the initial base was small, the current ranking structure of provincial industrial output may not be substantially different from that in the early 1950s.

One major phenomenon of Chinese industrial development in recent years has been a rapid expansion of small-scale or local industry, particularly in the rural areas. The current small industry policy differs from that in the Great Leap Forward (GLF) period in a number of important aspects. First, the primary thrust of small industry in the years following the GLF has been to serve agriculture. An increasingly large number of small industrial plants have been established under local administration throughout the countryside to provide agriculture with new or improved types of inputs. Second, absorption of surplus labor does not appear to be one of the major goals of the small industry policy today as it was in the GLF period. Local industry employs over 15 million workers, or only about 3 percent of total labor force. The American Rural Small-Scale Industries Delegation that visited China in the summer of 1974 found that there was, in fact, a shortage of labor for small plants in the Chinese countryside. Finally, the size of small plants today is generally larger than in the GLF period. Local or small-scale plants are not defined according to size, but pertain to those controlled by counties, communes, or brigades. Some have grown to a size that would no longer be small by international classification.

Small-scale industry in China is not an alternative to the development of medium- and large-scale plants, but rather plays a complementary role. Under current conditions

it can effectively utilize local resources, save transport
and marketing costs, and better understand and meet local
needs. Small-scale industry brings relatively modern
technology to the countryside, serving as a manufacturing
and managerial training ground for the peasants without
waiting for the spread of large-scale industrialization from
the urban centers. Thus, the gap between city and countryside is narrowed, providing not only economic advantages
but also long-term, positive implications for China's
social development.

Small-scale plants have expanded most rapidly in the
production of agricultural machinery, chemical fertilizers,
and cement and in the generation of hydroelectric power.[14]
The greatest significance is in the manufacture and repair
of agricultural equipment; these plants produced the lion's
share of such equipment in the PRC. Of China's twenty-nine
provinces, municipalities, and autonomous regions, twenty-
eight have established tractor manufacturing plants; facilities have been set up in 96 percent of the counties.

China's future industrial expansion will depend upon
certain basic principles of the Fifth FYP (1976-80), which
are reportedly under review. At least three sets of decisions are of fundamental importance. One of them is related
to the settling of investment priorities during the plan
period. During the Fourth FYP (1971-75) the petroleum industry was given a top priority in investment allocation. As
a result, crude oil output grew over 20 percent per year.
China's crude oil exports rose from negligible levels at
the beginning of the Fourth FYP to about 10 million tons
in 1975, yielding 850 million dollars of export income.
But the rate of growth of crude oil output began to decline
in the second half of 1975, and diminished further in
1976.[15] This decline reflects an intense debate within
the Chinese leadership about the allocation of investment
between the energy resources sector and other industries
and within the former, particularly petroleum vis-à-vis
coal. Involved in the debate was also the radicals'
attack on Teng Hsiao-p'ing for his alleged policy of indis-
criminate expansion of exporting industrial raw materials,
including crude oil, in exchange for foreign capital goods.
Toward the end of 1975 and early 1976 there probably was
a rearrangement of the order of industrial planning
priorities with the petroleum industry assigned a lower
relative position, perhaps after iron and steel and coal.

A second set of decisions has to do with the future of
China's technological policy. Chinese industry is still
dominated by inefficient production techniques, and a great
need exists to update and upgrade the state of industrial
technology. The PRC has long adopted a policy of technological dualism, known as "walking on two legs," in a form
of combining indigenous, labor-intensive innovations with

imported advanced technologies including technological
borrowing through licensing agreements, prototype copying,
scientific exchange, trade exhibits and associated technical seminars, and an intensive study of Western technical literature and product samples. The proper role of
foreign technology, however, has been frequently debated,
sometimes hotly. In the recent antirightist campaign,
there were attempts to minimize the role of foreign technology while placing stress on indigenous innovations
to be achieved through such means as three-in-one campaigns
and selecting workers for training in the so-called July
21 Universities established at the work sites. The Chinese
press recently has published detailed accounts as to how
the now discredited leaders opposed foreign trade, particularly complete plant imports. If China is to place greater
reliance on foreign technology, foreign trade will likely
expand.

And, last, a decision must be made on how to upgrade
conventional military forces. The People's Liberation
Army (PLA) is in great need of modernization. The Hua
regime, which relies heavily on the support of the military, will likely have to expand defense spending, in
response to increasing pressures from the PLA, reversing
the cutback of the early 1970s. But military modernization
will require huge resources for developing not only defense
industries but also those industries supporting defense
production such as steel, machine building, and electric
power, and therefore will have to compete against growing
investment requirements for civilian sectors (e.g., further industrialization, agricultural mechanization, transport expansion, increased production of consumer goods,
etc.). Four separate but related national conferences in
early 1977, attended by representatives of the PLA and
defense production sectors, reportedly discussed such
questions as defense modernization and the relationship
between the economy and the military establishment. These
conferences together with a major industrial conference to
be held this spring will probably help map out a strategy
of allocating resources between military and civilian needs.

These three sets of decisions are closely intertwined,
involving policies on economic development, technology and
equipment imports, and industrial raw material exports.
Peking planners presumably have an option of restructuring
these policies in a more progressive manner now that the
radical members have been removed from the leadership.
The new economic policy likely to grow out of the events
of 1976 will have a significant impact on the future course
of China's industrial development as well as its foreign
trade in years to come.

Foreign Trade

Although a relatively small sector of the Chinese economy, about 6 percent of gross national product, foreign trade has been used by the PRC as an important policy instrument for the pursuit of overall economic objectives. Imports of plant and equipment have constituted an important means of facilitating and accelerating industrial growth since China does not have the manufacturing capacity required to produce all of the capital goods needed. Such imports give the Chinese access to a wide spectrum of modern technology vital to an industrializing nation.

The PRC has relied on foreign trade to ease pressures on the domestic transport and distribution system and to improve the incentives and living standards of the population. The importation of grain since 1961 has contributed significantly to the food supply, particularly in coastal urban areas, and has eased the burden of transporting grain from the interior.[16] More importantly, foreign grain purchases have reduced the necessity to increase grain deliveries from China's own farmers, thus not adversely affecting their incentives to increase production.

Foreign trade permits compensation for shortfalls resulting from a decline in domestic production and from supply bottlenecks and planning errors. Years of inadequate investment in the iron ore and coal mining industries, for example, have retarded growth in steel and other key sectors of the economy. The recent importation of large quantities of mining equipment is directed toward easing this situation.

In dollar terms, China's foreign trade expanded from $4.3 billion in 1970 to $14 billion in 1974, but then leveled off. In 1975 China's exports rose 4 percent over 1974 to reach $6.9 billion while imports remained unchanged at the level of $7.4 billion. The dollar value of total trade in 1975 rose 2.1 percent over 1974, but the real value actually declined. Preliminary estimates show that China's trade with the nonsocialist countries may have dropped significantly this year, resulting in a decline in total trade in both monetary and real terms.

In general, the PRC has attempted to maintain a policy of an overall balance in trade, paying for imports with export earnings. Chinese imports and exports had generally kept in balance until 1974 when imports exceeded exports by $810 million, largely as a result of worldwide inflation and the economic recession in the West. In an effort to cut the trade deficit, some imports were reduced while others were financed by so-called deferred payments. Relatively good harvests in 1973 through 1975 also enabled China to sharply reduce the import of agricultural products. While imports still exceeded exports in 1975, the deficit

declined considerably to an estimate of $455 million.
Although early information suggests that China's trade last
year may have reached a balance or possibly even a small
surplus, debt service on complete plants and agricultural purchases should reduce the overall payments surplus
which China maintained in 1975.

In the first half of the 1970s, the commodity composition of China's foreign trade underwent some significant
changes. Of China's total imports, machinery and equipment
averaged about 20 percent in 1970-74, and rose to 30 percent
in 1975. An important aspect of such imports is the purchases of complete plants. The PRC contracted for $1.3
billion worth of complete plants in 1973 and about $800
million in 1974. Following the 1974 trade deficit, China's
purchases of complete plants slowed down markedly with 1975
contracts estimated at $382.4 million. As of October, more
than $170 million of complete plant contracts had been
signed in 1976.

Minerals and metals accounted for about 15 percent of
all imports during 1970-73, and rose to 26 percent in 1974
and 29 percent in 1975, with ferrous ores and metals,
dominated by finished steel, making up more than three quarters of the category.[17]

Chemicals products averaged about 10 percent of China's
total imports in recent years. Fertilizers have been the
most important component of chemical imports, but their
relative importance has been declining gradually and will
continue to do so as the foreign-built ammonia-urea complexes come on-stream in 1976-77.

Grain imports dropped from the peak level of 7.7
million tons in 1973 and 7 million tons in 1974 to 3.3
million tons in 1975. Imports in 1976 declined further
to some 2 million tons. Imports in 1976 declined further
to some 2 million tons. The import of cotton, another
major agricultural commodity purchased in significant quantities, reached the peak level of 423,000 tons in 1973,
and declined in 1974-75 because of slow demand for Chinese
textiles. Toward the end of 1975, with world textile
markets improving and a reduced domestic output of raw
cotton, China again became active in the market, buying
from Mediterranean, African, and Latin American sources.[18]

About half of Chinese sales abroad are derived from
foodstuffs and raw materials of agricultural and animal
origin, with rice becoming an increasingly important
export item. Now a major rice-exporting country, China
is selling 1.5 to 2 million tons a year to over sixty
countries.

The growing importance of oil exports has caused a
decline in recent years in the relative share of foodstuffs and raw materials. China had been an oil importer,
but has become self-sufficient in petroleum with some

surplus for exports. Crude oil exports in significant quantities began in 1973, with the share of petroleum and petroleum products rising from less than 2 percent in 1973 to 8 percent in 1974 and 11 percent in 1975.

Intermediate and finished textile products accounted for about 25 percent of Chinese exports during 1970-75. In that period, increasingly large quantities of a wide variety of other manufactured consumer goods were sold to foreign countries. Machinery and equipment, mostly shipped to Third World countries, made up 4 to 5 percent of total exports.

China's exports of chemicals, minerals, and metals remained steady in their relative share during the first half of the 1970s, with chemicals accounting for 4 to 6 percent of total exports and minerals and metals about 4 percent.

In recent years China has increased its participation in international trade events. It participated in multinational trade fairs, mostly in Europe, Africa, and the Near East, organized its own exhibitions abroad, mostly in Pacific Basin countries, Africa, and Latin America, and allowed other countries to hold an increasing number of exhibitions with emphasis on technologically advanced industrial displays. Additionally, China held a number of minifairs for selected products in various cities to supplement the semiannual trade fair in Canton.

One significant development of China's foreign trade in recent years has been the rapid expansion of the transport system, especially the merchant navy and port facilities, needed to support greatly expanded imports and exports. About 80 percent of the foreign trade moves by sea and, although the larger share of this is carried in chartered bottoms, that share is declining as the Chinese merchant fleet expands. At the present time, China's merchant navy, which hardly existed in 1963, is one of the biggest in the world, with an estimated total of 4.5 million deadweight tons (dwt).[19]

Merchant navy growth has been achieved both by development of the domestic shipbuilding industry and by acquisition of ships abroad. Merchant ship output nearly tripled between 1970 and 1975.[20] New ships have been purchased from Bulgaria, East Germany, Finland, Japan, Rumania, and Yugoslavia, but most purchases have been used vessels, usually ten to fifteen years old, bought for refitting in Chinese yards.[21]

With the growth of the merchant marine has come a rapid expansion of China's congested, relatively shallow, major seaports. Increased traffic has entailed the deepening of channels, construction of new storage and handling facilities, and development of new rail connections.[22] When ongoing harbor projects are complete, the loading and unloading capacity of coastal ports will increase 50 percent over 1972, and more than double the 1965 level;

cargo-handling capacity added in the period 1972-75 is
believed to be about 60-70 million tons. While much of
the cargo-handling capacity is now said to be at least
partially mechanized, the PRC has only just begun con-
tainerized shipments.[23]
        Concurrent with the expansion of major ports, new oil-
handling facilities and pipelines have been constructed to
serve oil exports. The 1,507-km, 24-inch crude transmission
line linking the Taching oilfield to the port of Chinhuangtao
was completed in 1974. More recently, this line has been
extended to the Peking refinery. Another 24-inch line starting at Taching has been completed and brings crude to the new
oil port at Talien. Thus, Taching oil may now be delivered
in amounts of around 20-25 million tons to Talien for export,
although some of this would no doubt be siphoned off for
refinery input.[24]
        All in all, China's foreign trade developments since
1970 have shown that the PRC has no inclination of pursuing
a totally autarkic course of economic development. And,
although the late Chairman Mao on numerous occasions
stressed the need for self-reliance, he also added that
China should learn from other countries. In the first half
of the 1970s, this has allowed for substantial imports of
foreign plant and technology ($2.5 billion in 1973-75) as
well as agricultural products. Although contracts for
these imports slackened in 1975-76 partly because of the
radicals' opposition to heavy reliance on foreign technology and equipment, the prospect for the future has been
brightened considerably by an open stance on foreign trade
taken by the newly realigned leadership. If such an
attitude persists, China's imports, particularly in areas
of advanced technology, will expand. In the next two or
three years, however, the expansion is likely to be slow.
        In the final analysis, the level of China's imports
depends basically on its capability to generate export
earnings. A promising source of such earnings lies in the
much publicized crude oil, but its export potential may be
significantly constrained by increasing domestic requirements for energy necessitated by industrialization and
agricultural mechanization. Another major source of export
income could be derived from increased sales of Chinese
rice, textiles, and other labor-intensive industrial products. China is the world's leading producer of rice;
with good harvests rice exports could exceed 2 million
tons annually. But cotton textiles are currently rationed
in China, and there are definite limits to the expansion
of other commodities that Peking can find to market.
        To help pay for imports, China in recent years has
adopted a limited use of commercial credit. Short-term
commercial credit has been used to purchase foreign goods;
five-year credits financed by Japanese and European

governmental banks have been used to buy complete plants;
and interbank deposits at market interest rates have been
accepted. The extended use of commercial credit, however,
will be prohibited by debt service obligations already
acquired. Most of the complete plant contracts which China
signed with the West in 1973-75 call for an initial payment
after the delivery of equipment and machinery and for a payment schedule thereafter covering a number of years. China
will have to make large repayments throughout the years
1976-80, with a peak in 1977-78.

To conclude, the level of China's foreign trade in the
balance of the decade will probably continue to rise as in
the early 1970s, but the rate of growth will be strongly
influenced by Peking's ability or willingness to increase
exports, particularly oil, and to obtain Western credits, by
the type of economic development called for in the Fifth
FYP, by the state of the world economy, and by whether
China experiences any natural disasters such as those
plaguing the country in 1976.

Human Resources

A number of population and labor issues will affect the
future course of China's economic development. There is no
general agreement on the precise magnitude of the Chinese
population. A Western estimate puts the Chinese population
in 1975 at 935 million.[25] The PRC has not officially
published detailed population estimates since the late
1950s. In recent months, twenty-one provinces in their
condolences of Mao's death and salutatory messages to Hua
reported population figures. These figures, together with
earlier Chinese sources published for the other seven provinces, suggest that the Chinese population at the present
time is probably in the neighborhood of 900 million.[26] At
the same time, a top Chinese official was reported to have
said in late 1976 that the Chinese population was slightly
above 800 million.[27]

Chinese officials have openly acknowledged the inaccu-
racy of their population statistics. Deputy Premier Li
Hsien-nien once said that different agencies used different
sets of population estimates to suit their planning objectives.[28] More recently, a report has revealed the existence
of a tendency on the part of various provinces to conceal
deaths in order to obtain more rations of grain, clothing,
and other goods.[29] Mao was also reported to have made the
same point. He spoke additionally of double counting
arising from the fact that many people changed their resi-
dence several times without making proper registration.[30]

Official statistics published for the 1950s show that
China's population grew at an average rate of 2.2 percent
a year. No data on the population growth have become

available since the late 1950s. A drive to reduce births
was begun in the mid-1960s. Birth control clinics have
been established, and contraception has been made readily
available. Strong economic and social pressures have been
brought to bear on young people to prevent marriage below
prescribed ages. There appears to have been a considerable
decline in the birthrate where these programs were undertaken, but the traditional desire to have more children
has not been completely overcome, especially in the countryside. At the same time, improved nutrition and progress
in public health have reduced death rates. The rate of
population growth in recent years probably has not been
significantly lower than that in the 1950s.
    Assume that the present size of the Chinese population
is in the range of 850-900 million and that it will grow at
an annual rate of close to 2 percent. This means that a
new population equivalent in size to the entire population
of the state of California will have been created each year
in China. Such addition to the already large population in
China would impose a tremendous burden on the agricultural
sector which, as indicated above, is not likely to grow
rapidly. Under normal harvest conditions, increases in
grain production will probably be sufficient only to feed
additional mouths without an adequate surplus to support
an ambitious industrialization program. The success of
China's modernization efforts, therefore, will depend
critically on its ability to reduce the rate of population
growth.
    Further, the large cohorts of young workers generated
by population increases will have to be absorbed into productive employment. China appears to have achieved high
employment levels. But the bulk of the labor force is
engaged in low-productivity employment. The problem for
China, therefore, is not only to create new means of absorb-
ing additional labor in production but, more importantly,
to raise the productivity of the existing and newly employed
labor.
    Labor productivity can be raised through improvements
in the quality of labor, which in turn may be achieved by,
among other means, improved health care, better education
and research, and greater stress on material incentives.
China has made remarkable progress in public health,
especially in rural areas where 80 percent of the population
lives. The number of hospitals and clinics run by the
communes and brigades have increased greatly, even though
by Western standards their facilities are still primitive.
A distinct feature of China's rural health program is the
use of a large number of "barefoot doctors." Given the
severe shortage of qualified physicians, the barefoot doctors have performed a useful function in the delivery of
basic medical and health services to millions of peasants.

Yet the system of barefoot doctors, which has by no means been an unqualified success as the Chinese press seems to claim, can be improved greatly.[31] The system is mainly a stopgap measure rather than a permanent solution to the short supply of physicians. To improve public health in the long run, many more formally trained doctors will be required.

Education and scientific research had been one of the focal points in the internal debate until the recent shakeup in the leadership. The radicals placed heavy emphasis on "redness," i.e., on the political and ideological attitude of the students and their willingness to serve the revolution. They attempted to downgrade the system of examination and certain traditional roles of universities and technical institutes. The minister of education who supported more traditional institutions was under severe attack and was subsequently ousted from office. Long-term, basic scientific and technical research has long been deemphasized in China. As mentioned earlier, in recent years the PRC has relied on the so-called July 21 Universities organized by factory workers as one of the principal ways to enhance technical skills in industry and on the mass line approach to agricultural scientific research by scattering millions of farmer-scientists at the grassroots level. The failure to develop both higher education and long-range, theoretical research will severely limit China's capability to improve the human capital which, as the experiences of developed countries show, is the most important source of economic growth.

Raising material incentives probably will have a more immediate effect on output than improving public health, education, and research. Per capita real consumption in China has gradually risen, more rapidly in the countryside than in the cities. The government has tried to avoid taking measures which would have an adverse impact on farm production. Therefore, the production team of only twenty to forty households has remained as a rule the accounting unit in the commune structure, thus not separating further the relationship between effort and income. No serious attempts have been made to abolish or reduce the private plots that provide Chinese peasants a major source of supplementary income. A most interesting aspect of China's agricultural incentive policy, as Dwight Perkins has hypothesized, is to import grain for the purpose of encouraging production.[32] In recent years, relatively small fluctuations in China's grain harvests, less than 5 percent, have been accommodated by very large swings, nearly 100 percent, in foreign grain purchases. This policy has the effect of stabilizing the farmer's obligations to turn over his output to the procurement agency, thus not dampening his incentive to increase production.

Chinese peasants also have benefited from the government policy to narrow the gap between income in the rural
and urban areas. The prices of agricultural products have
risen more rapidly than the prices of industrial products.
In some cases, the prices of products purchased by farmers
have fallen. Peasant consumption has also improved due to
increases in services provided by the state.

On the other hand, average wages of industrial workers
have improved very little since the late 1950s. This has
given rise to widespread discontent among urban workers.
The problem became serious in 1974, when labor unrest in
many plants caused production to fall off. A national conference on wages, which had been scheduled for the early
part of this year presumably to discuss, among other things,
possible pay raises for industrial workers, was canceled
because of the opposition of the radicals. Chinese workers,
who have generally expressed their ill-feeling toward Chiang
Ch'ing and her radical colleagues, probably are hoping for
some wage increases and bonuses for good work. One of the
most pressing tasks faced by the Hua administration, therefore, is to solve the issue of wages and incentives. The
problem, however, is not an easy one. Aside from the ideological paradox of material motivation and China's long-held
policy of gradually reducing urban-rural income differentials,
large investment requirements for modernization programs
will not permit a significant wage increase. But even a
small general increase may help improve motivation and raise
productivity.

Conclusion

The Chinese economy has developed unevenly since the
founding of the People's Republic. Ideology and political
campaigns have played a major role in the erratic development. Some students of the Chinese economy postulate that
China's economic development seems to have followed a
cyclical pattern. Several years of considerable economic
progress were usually followed by increasing emphasis on
ideology and by intensified campaigns to implement ideology.
Stress on ideology in turn frequently led to economic
declines or slowdowns, and then to a relaxation of ideology
and campaigns.

Chinese experiences demonstrate clearly that ideology
in its extreme form and sustained economic growth cannot coexist. Indeed, ideological extremism in China is in sharp
conflict with economic rationality. At the present time,
there are indications of some ideological relaxation.
One such indication is seen in the first official revelation
of Mao's 1956 speech, "Ten Great Relations," which outlines
moderate economic approaches to development in contrast

to the radical policies pursued during the Great Leap Forward and the Cultural Revolution. If this trend continues,
the prospect is for economic expansion in the balance of
the 1970s. Perhaps there will be substantial rates of
aggregate output growth, continuing high employment levels,
some expansion of high-technology plant and equipment imports
and raw material exports, modest progress in labor productivity, a small increase in per capita consumption, and a
slight decline in the rate of population growth.
      But a more fundamental question is whether China will
be able to get away from the cyclical pattern of development now that Mao is gone. If the PRC is to achieve its
goal of evolving into a truly first-rate economic power by
the end of the century, it cannot afford to have another
Cultural Revolution in the process. It would appear that
some aspects of Maoist ideology would have to be discarded,
or at least greatly compromised. This probably will be the
most formidable test for the leadership in post-Mao China.

                              Notes

      1. The joint editorial of the People's Daily, Red
Flag, and the Liberation Army Daily, published on Oct. 25,
1976, declares, "We will certainly be able ... to totally
achieve within the present century the modernization of
agriculture, industry, national defense, and science and
technology to build our country into a socialist power"
(Jen-min jih-pao [People's Daily], Oct. 25, 1976, p. 4).
      2. Dwight H. Perkins, "Constraints Influencing
China's Agricultural Performance," in China: A Reassessment of the Economy, Joint Economic Committee, U.S. Congress, (Washington, D.C.: U.S. Government Printing Office,
1975), p. 365.
      3. The estimate does not include soybeans. The out-
put of soybeans increased from 14.9 million tons in 1974 to
17 million tons in 1975. All tons in this chapter are
metric.
      4. The multiple cropping index, i.e., the ratio of
sown acreage to cultivated acreage, rose from 131% in
1952 to 145% in 1958 when official statistics of multiple
cropping ceased. One independent estimate puts the index
at 150 for 1966, and it has probably continued to rise
in recent years. Recent Chinese press reports indicate
that China's double crop acreage in 1974 rose by nearly
200% over the early 1950s and that in many areas the
multiple cropping index rose greatly in 1975.
      5. In addition to multiple cropping of the same crop
during growing periods, intercropping of different crops
has become an increasingly important practice in China.

The American Plant Studies Delegation, which visited
China in the fall of 1974, found that intercropping was
widely adopted in most of the areas visited, such as
Kwangtung, Kiangsu, Kirin, and Shensi provinces and the
Shanghai area. However, there was little intercropping
in the Yellow River Valley where rainfall deficiency limits
crop growth.
        6. In 1973, for example, the world average of fer-
tilizer use was 53 kg/ha, and the Japanese rate was 425
kg/ha.
        7. For centuries the Chinese farmer has preserved
soil fertility through the traditional use of such organic
manures as night soil, stable manure, compost, green
manure, crop residues, mud matter, and oil cakes. One
estimate put the availability of nitrogenous nutrients from
organic fertilizers in 1956 at 3.8 million tons, or 34
kg/ha. Pig manure alone probably contributed 10 kg/ha.
Another estimate indicated that the plant nutrients derived
from natural sources amounted to 39 kg/ha in 1965. By the
early 1970s, the per hectare average of nitrogen available
from night soil and pig and other stable manures probably
had risen to at least 55 kg.
        8. According to one report, Chinese surveys found
that about one-half of the farmland in Hopei, Honan, and
Shantung provinces could eventually be brought under
irrigation by wells. A more recent report, released in
February 1976, indicated that about half of the farmland
in these provinces had been brought under irrigation.
These two reports, taken together, suggest that the irrigated area in these provinces cannot be expanded much
farther.
        9. Between 1970 and 1975 powered irrigation and
drainage pump capacity rose from 16.9 to 43 million horsepower. By comparison, pumping capacity was only 560,000
horsepower in 1957, 5.8 million horsepower in 1962, and
8.45 million horsepower in 1965.
        10. It was reported in 1972 in the Chinese press
that state fixed investment in industry in the early
1970s was several times the total amount of state revenue
in the early 1950s.
        11. Unless otherwise noted, industrial statistics
in this section are based on People's Republic of China:
Handbook of Economic Indicators, CIA Research Aid, Aug.
1976.
        12. Ching-chi tao-pao [Economic Reporter], no. 29
(July 28, 1976), p. 3.
        13. There were many reports in the Chinese press,
published in November 1976, attributing the "loss" of
production to the interference by the "Gang of Four."
        14. In certain regions there also have been large
increases in the number of small coal and iron ore mines,

small iron and steel mills, electronics plants, and food-processing centers. Currently, small-scale industry prob-ably accounts for 30% of China's coal output, 20% of the pig iron, and 15% of the crude steel.

15.   China's crude oil output grew 24% in the first half of 1975 (over the comparable period in 1974), while the rate of growth for the entire year of 1975 was only 13.3%. The growth rate declined to 12.7% in the first quarter of 1976, and to 10.3% in the second quarter of the same year. For 1976 as a whole, the rate of growth was 13%.

16.   So, too, has the import of oil in South China even though an exportable surplus exists in the North.

17.   Nonferrous metal imports were led by copper, nickel, aluminum, and lead. Aluminum imports rose sharply in 1975, when China signed purchase contracts for about 350,000 tons at a cost of some $270 million.

18.   A third agricultural commodity, which China has imported regularly, is raw sugar. Imports in 1975 fell below the 1974 volume of 630,000 tons, perhaps to half a million tons.

19.   The figure includes only ocean-going vessels using the international seaways and not coastal ships.

20.   China's output of major and minor vessels rose from 169 million dwt in 1970 to 494.2 million dwt in 1975. Of the total output in 1975, major vessels accounted for 308.2 million dwt and minor vessels 186 million dwt.

21.   Between 1969 and mid-1974, 64 used ships of 1,114,000 dwt were obtained from Norwegian, British, West German, Swedish, Greek, and Japanese sources.

22.   In some 17 major ports along the coast there are about 260 berths, of which about 80 are deepwater slips capable of accommodating 10,000-ton or larger ships; the new port at Talien can bring 100,000-dwt tankers along-side. Over half of the deepwater berths were completed between 1973 and 1975.

23.   The construction of a container terminal in Hsinkang had nearly been completed before the earthquake in July 1976. It is not clear to what extent the quake may have caused damages to the terminal. Another terminal is in operation in Shanghai where 20- and 40-foot con-tainers are handled.

24.   Two other pipelines have been constructed. One connects the Shengli field to the Shangtung oil port of Huangtao; the other--of undetermined, but probably small, size--links Taching with North Korea. According to a New China News Agency report, the total length of oil pipelines laid in China in the past decade was 8 times that for all the years before 1965.

25.   People's Republic of China: Handbook of Economic Indicators, CIA Research Aid, Aug. 1976.

26.   The population figures in millions for 21

PART II

Patterns and Prospects of U.S.-China Trade

3. China's Foreign Trade: Principles, Institutions, and Performance

Eugene A. Theroux

Confucius once asked happily "Is it not delightful to have friends coming from distant quarters?"[1] That sentiment may be one of the many reasons the sage is in disrepute in China, for the Chinese by tradition have not felt moved to throw open the gates to foreigners, and particularly not to foreign traders.

Chinese attitudes were perhaps more accurately reflected by Emperor Ch'ien Lang. Having received a request from His Royal Highness, King George III, for a trade mission to China, the emperor replied: "Our Celestial Empire possesses all things in prolific abundance and lacks no product within its borders. Therefore, there is no need to import the manufacturers of outside barbarians."

Once China had been pried open to foreign trade, the effects justified the emperor's forebodings. China's vice-minister of foreign trade has described the nineteenth-century experience with the West this way:

> For over a century, the imperialistic powers divided China into their spheres of influence, interfered in China's internal affairs, backed the reactionary authorities, subjected the Chinese people's revolutionary struggle to bloody suppression, engineered civil wars among warlords, controlled China's customs, shipping and insurance, manipulated China's financial and monetary affairs, extorted privileges of running mines and factories, building railways, engaging in inland navigation.

> They flagrantly plundered China's resources, fleeced the Chinese people and seriously disrupted the national economy. Rural areas were on the brink of bankruptcy. Its own industry was moribund. Major necessities like grain and cotton had to be imported in large quantities. China's entire foreign trade was in the hands of imperialists and their running dogs.[2]

Not surprisingly, the Chinese since liberation have proved wary of the potentiality trade has for the disruption and exploitation of China. Consequently, they try to conduct foreign trade on the basis of fundamental principles.

China's Foreign Trade Principles

As Americans have discovered in the five years since the Shanghai Communiqué, Chinese rhetoric is different from our own. It seems to us to be turgid, excessively political,

and repetitious. And, therefore, few besides scholars
and government analysts scrutinize very carefully the
texts of official Chinese statements, editorials, and
maxims. Often, those who do peruse Chinese periodicals
disregard what the Chinese say--about foreign trade, for
example--as impossible gobbledygook, unworthy of serious
attention.

It has been my experience, in doing business with
the Chinese, that they do not waste words. Furthermore,
I have found their official statements to be unfailing
(if sometimes changing) signals along the sometimes tor-
tuous paths of trade. What the Chinese say about trade
and development is ignored by an American businessman at
his peril, for by the principles they enunciate and the
priorities they set the businessman can gauge his business
prospects fairly accurately.

Are the Chinese today interested in foreign trade,
or do they subscribe to the views of Emperor Ch'ien Lang?
We have no less an authority than Chairman Mao himself on
this question: "The Chinese people wish to have friendly
cooperation with the people of all countries and to resume
and expand international trade in order to develop production and promote economic prosperity."

But the Chinese people's wishes in this respect are
not to be realized by individual Chinese entrepreneurs.
The Chinese businessmen who thrived under the Kuomintang
are gone and unlamented. Trade in China since 1949 has
had exclusively state purposes whose achievement are sought
through the apparatus of the state. Chairman Mao has said:
"The restoration and development of the national economy
of the people's republic would be impossible without a
policy of controlling foreign trade."

Trade is controlled by both principles of proper
trade behavior and a bureaucracy which conducts trade
according to those principles. Though variously stated
by the Chinese, the main principles of foreign trade are
two:

1. Trade must be conducted on the basis of equality
and mutual benefit, and

2. the purpose of trade is to make China more
self-reliant.[3]

The Shanghai Joint Communiqué of February 27, 1972,
makes reference to the first of these two points: "Both
sides view bilateral trade as another area from which
mutual benefit can be derived, and agreed that economic
relations based on equality and mutual benefit are in
the interest of the peoples of the two countries."

Li Chiang, China's minister of foreign trade, cited
this same principle not long ago: "As is widely known,
China has persistently adhered to the policy of equality,
mutual benefit and helping to meet each other's needs in

trade with other countries. It is a policy determined by
the nature of our socialist system."4 What does "equality
and mutual benefit" mean to China? It means no unequal
trade agreements. It means no discrimination against
Chinese products in foreign markets. It means China will
purchase on fair terms only and will resist overreaching
by the foreigner, but it recognizes that in fair trade
both sides benefit. And trade has important noncommercial
by-products, too. This theme is summarized in a booklet
published in Peking and widely circulated abroad:

> Liberation deprived imperialism of every
> prerogative in China, changed the situation
> of hanging on the coat tails of imperialism
> in foreign trade by old China, and started the
> country on the road of independent foreign trade
> free from outside control, to serve the socialist
> construction. Foreign trade has become an impor-
> tant means of exchanging goods on the basis of
> equality and mutual benefit, as well as of
> exchanging experience, learning from each other,
> promoting friendship and understanding between
> the Chinese people and the peoples of the
> world.5

For the would-be exporter to China, there is no more
important Chinese principle affecting trade than that of
self-reliance. It is a principle which is rooted firmly
in the Chinese Revolution and nourished in the bitter experience that outsiders, from the predatory foreign merchants
and bankers of the nineteenth century to the Soviet advisors of the twentieth, can never be counted upon to help
China. Chairman Mao wrote in 1945: "We stand for self-
reliance. We hope for foreign aid but cannot be dependent
on it; we depend on our own efforts, on the creative power
of the whole army and the entire people."6 Later, Chairman
Mao expressed the principle this way: "Rely mainly on our own
efforts while making external assistance subsidiary, break
down blind faith, go in for industry, agriculture and
technical and cultural revolutions independently, do away
with slavishness, bury dogmatism, learn from the good
experience of other countries conscientiously and be sure
to study their bad experience too, so as to draw lessons
from it. This is our line."
The preamble of China's new constitution also empha-
sizes the chairman's instructions: "We should build
socialism independently and with the initiative in our own
hands, through self-reliance, hard struggle, diligence
and thrift and by going all out, aiming high and achieving
greater, faster, better and more economical results."
The minister of foreign trade has explained the fundamental character of the self-reliance principle:

Upon the founding of New China in 1949, we at
once abolished all the privileges enjoyed by the
imperialists in old China and held the lifelines
of our national economy tightly in our own hands.
Thus we thoroughly demolished old China's dependence upon imperialism for foreign trade and set
up a new-type independent sovereign foreign trade
to serve the interests of our socialist construction. We maintain that a country's political
sovereignty cannot be separated from its economic
independence. After obtaining political independence, a nation must strive hard to win economic independence, otherwise the achieved political independence is unconsolidated and incomplete. Over
the past twenty years under the leadership of
Chairman Mao Tsetung and the Communist Party of
China, the Chinese people have persisted in the
policy of maintaining independence, keeping the
initiative in their own hands and self-reliance
in socialist construction. That is to say starting
from actual conditions by relying on the strength
and wisdom of the people, through domestic accumulation of funds and making full use of China's own
natural resources they have transformed an old,
poor and backward China into a socialist country
with initial prosperity.[7]

Although the trade minister has affirmed that "we
adhere to the policy of maintaining independence, keeping
the initiative in our own hands and relying on our own
efforts," he has also pointed out that "under no circumstances does it mean pursuing a 'closed door' policy":

Over the last two decades and more, acting upon
this teaching of Chairman Mao on foreign trade,
China has opened up trade with other countries
of the world in a planned way, on the basis of
equality and mutual benefit, to learn from other
countries' merits and obtain necessary materials,
equipment and techniques through exchange. This
is an implementation of the principle of making
foreign things serve China, and combining learning
with inventing in order to add to our ability to
build socialism independently and with the initiative in our own hands through self-reliance to
speed up the pace of our socialist construction.
Facts prove that foreign trade is necessary to the
development of our national economy.[8] (Emphasis
added.)

Peking's interest in and need for advanced goods and
techniques from abroad is undeniable. But so are the
evident pressures from those Chinese who, for reasons of

politics, ideology, or economic priorities, oppose such
transactions as violative of the objective of self-reliance. Recurring Chinese rhetoric, in fact, seems to strain
to satisfy all sides of the continuing domestic debate
over to the extent to which China should purchase abroad.
     Jen-Min jih-Pao (People's Daily), for example, has
editorialized: "We rely on our own hands to equip ourselves
technically. The introduction of some essential new equipment and techniques is also for implementing the principle of making foreign things serve China and linking
study with original creation so as to promote better self-
reliance and accelerate the building of socialism." The
same newspaper, China's most important, recently reminded
the Chinese people:

> The erroneous notion of blind faith in the
> "advanced" technology of foreign countries still
> exists among some of the comrades...they see only
> the foreign countries, and seek only to import
> things...if they are permitted to have their way,
> they would take the evil road of revisionism...
> [but] in emphasizing adhering to the policy of
> maintaining independence and keeping the initia-
> tive in our own hands and relying on our own
> efforts, we do not mean discriminating against
> learning from foreign countries...[we should]
> absorb whatever experience is useful to us...
> the introduction of a bit of foreign technology
> is permissible.

     Still more recently, the influential Shanghai theore-
tical monthly Hsueh-shi yu pi-pan (Study and Self-Criticism)
excoriated some Chinese for "worshipping things foreign"--
those "who think the moon is rounder abroad." The journal
directed its attack specifically at "certain servile lackeys
of imperialism" working to "hawk the ideology that Chinese
industry is incapable of developing without technical aid
from abroad." It asked: "Did not China launch atomic
bombs and artificial satellites in the sky, one after
another, depending on our own abilities?"
     The radical journal Hung ch'i (Red Flag) published in
its April 1976 issue an article severely criticizing certain
wrong tendencies in China's foreign trade. The article,
entitled "Criticize Comprador Philosophy," attacks the idea
of increasing exports for the purpose of obtaining "more
good things from abroad." Exporting "in an unprincipled
manner" simply for the sake of exports would jeopardize
China's economic and political independence. Such a policy,
the article argues, could cause China to import goods
which could be domestically produced, foster export of
items needed at home, cause purchase of advanced products
while perpetuating domestic production of backward goods,

and even cause surrender over exploitation of mineral resources.

The "tilt" against broadened foreign trade, evident in the Hung ch'i article, changed dramatically by March 1977. It is now clear that Hung ch'i in April 1976 was one of the voices of the "Gang of Four"--a clique at that time successfully opposing the "arch unrepentent capitalist-roader Teng Hsiao-ping" among whose "errors" was a policy to finance imports of foreign capital goods, plants, and technology out of proceeds from increased petroleum sales. A recent article by China's "foreign trade workers," appearing in January 1977, tilts the other way. It charges that two of the four Gang members, Chang Ch'un-ch'iao and Yao Wen-yüan, "used newspapers and journals under their control to put out a spate of reactionary articles to confuse the general public. They published, among others, an article entitled 'Criticize Philosophy of Servility to Things Foreign' in a journal, charging the Ministry of Foreign Trade with 'national betrayal and surrender, running China mainly by begging from other countries.'"[9]

The Chinese press in early 1977 is, in fact, full of severe criticism for those who, only a year before, took China's trade principles to mean the greatest possible degree of autarky. Now, as in the article just quoted, the autarkist Gang of Four and its followers are vehemently accused of being "ignorant of economic, trade and foreign affairs," and of "undermining foreign trade."

Like any broad principles, then, those we have discussed will be variously interpreted and applied, depending upon changing emphasis at higher political levels. That, in turn, will depend on who is in charge, and the nature of China's needs at the time. Consider two recent examples, not untypical of those American businessmen are now confronting.

The Case of Peking Motor Vehicles Plant No. 2

Does China need or want foreign trucks? As the world's premier producers of motor vehicles, Americans have naturally considered the potential of such a market in China. In fact, the Chinese have bought a few large and very specialized U.S.-built trucks. But will the evident transport needs of China be met with imports or by self-reliance? One not very encouraging sign comes in the form of a 1976 article from a Chinese publication entitled "Auto Workers Criticize Teng's Slavish Comprador Philosophy":

Indignation among the workers of the Peking No. 2 Motor Vehicles Plant was aroused when the arch

unrepentant Party capitalist-roader Teng Hsiao-
ping stirred up a Right deviationist wind around
last summer and peddled once again the slavish
comprador philosophy and gradualism which had been
criticized in the early stage of the Cultural
Revolution. He went so far as to attempt to
cut down China's own productivity and import
foreign equipment and products, actions which
would turn China into a raw material supplier
of imperialism and social imperialism.

The workers pointed out that Teng Hsiao-ping's
line was just the same as Liu Shao-chi's. The
plant had trial-produced a small platform truck
before the Cultural Revolution. But the few
"experts" who monopolized the designing so
venerated what was foreign that they refused
to consider the workers' good suggestions.

In the current anti-Right deviationist struggle,
the workers recounted the tremendous successes the
plant had achieved since the start of the Cultural
Revolution and said: these successes are attributable to Chairman Mao's policy of "maintaining independence and keeping the initiative in our own
hands and relying on our own efforts" and to our
efforts in criticizing the slavish comprador philosophy.

In 1966 when the Cultural Revolution began, the
plant again took up the task of trial-producing the
small platform truck. The workers were determined
that they would complete the undertaking through
self-reliance in accordance with Chairman Mao's
revolutionary line.

Design groups made up of workers, leading
cadres and technicians were set up. They were
opposed to the idea of copying a foreign model,
and on analysing and studying an imported truck
pointed out a number of shortcomings. The designing groups turned to the workers for their
opinions.... After four months' hard work, they
succeeded in turning out two sample trucks....

When the model 130 small platform truck went
into mass production, some people influenced by
Liu Shao-chi's revisionist line spread word
that it was too expensive to make and would be
cheaper to import. The workers criticized this
erroneous view and said with pride: "We must
take the road of independence and not trail along
after foreigners." High costs was a passing
phenomenon in trial-manufacturing, the workers
pointed out. They were determined to turn out
more trucks on their own and to cut the production
costs....

In the course of mass producing and expanding the production of the truck, workers, leading
cadres and technicians of the plant did not ask
the state for equipment, factory buildings or
funds. They adhered to the spirit of self-reliance
and transformed the existing equipment at hand.
They went all out to make technical innovations.

With Teng's detractors now under arrest, themselves
the objects of a thoroughgoing national campaign of vilifi-
cation and ridicule, and with the prospect of a Teng "comeback" being taken seriously, how should the philosophy
expressed in the foregoing article, be understood today by
American firms interested in exporting capital goods,
plants, or technology to China?

The Case of the Nanking Radio Factory

Importers, too, must be conscious of China's trade principles and practices. The enormous productive potential of
China's millions of workers has not been lost on American
importers or manufacturers of light manufactured goods.
Many of them, computing the capacity of the Chinese work
force with the relatively low cost of Chinese labor, fore-
see China as a kind of postwar Japan. It is on the verge,
they calculate, of providing colossal quantities of certain kinds of goods--textiles, toys, sporting goods, house-
wares, consumer electronic products, handicrafts, and the
like--of high quality and at low cost. Moreover, they
hope the Chinese will do as other Far East manufacturers
have been eager to do, namely, build products to U.S.
specifications, suitable for U.S. consumer tastes, and
under private U.S. brand names.
Such may happen. There was some reason to believe
this might develop soon, when Sino-U.S. trade began to
increase markedly in 1973 and 1974. But recent signs
indicate that the principles of equality and self-reliance
are today interpreted in such a manner that many American
firms will have to buy on Chinese terms or not buy at all:

China's giant panda is the trade mark of
radios made by the Nanking Radio Factory--
radios very different from the Philco radio
this same factory used to assemble before
liberation.
Lao Huang, a worker in the factory before
liberation, is chairman of the revolutionary
committee. "All our factory did in the old
days," he told me, "was assemble radios with
U.S. parts for the Philco Company and sell
them in China. The factory was set up by

Kuomintang bureaucrat-capital. We workers called
the radios 'slave models with foreign parts and
foreign style.' We wanted to design and make
Chinese radios--only a dream in semi-colonial and
semi-feudal China. Once a Chinese engineer
designed a case which looked better than the
imported one. But it had to be sent to the
Philco Company for approval and, of course,
it was turned down. The factory was a typical
colonial enterprise."

After Nanking was liberated in April 1949,
workers became masters in the factory. Now
led by the Communist Party and Chairman Mao,
they produced the Red Star radio and other new
products needed by the country with materials
and parts made in China. Facing the imperialists' blockade, they overcame the difficulties in the spirit of self-reliance and hard
work.

On January 11, 1956, Chairman Mao, great
leader of the Chinese people, visited the Nanking
Radio Factory. He praised the workers for stick-
ing to the policy of self-reliance in design and
manufacture. This fired the workers with a
determination to put out more and better products to serve the socialist motherland.

That was the year they designed and produced
the first Panda radio. Since then, design and
quality have constantly improved so that Panda
radios are one of the most popular in the country....

"The changes from assembling Philcos to making
Pandas," Chairman Lao Huang said, "made us see
that revolution can change everything. Once
the people become masters of their own fate and
rely on their own strength, they can create
anything."...

During the cultural revolution when mental
shackles were being broken, the workers decided
to make a semi-automatic assembling and end-
cutting machine. Two ways of looking at it came
out: design their own or copy foreign ones.
The copyists said, "If we fail, all we'll have
is a heap of scrap and lose more than we'll
gain." Most of the workers were for self-
reliance. "When we do our own cooking," they
said, "we have what we like to eat. When we
build a road, it goes where we want it to go.
Copying foreign machines will make us dependent on foreign countries. We'll blaze our
own trail...."

Workers of the Nanking Radio Factory are

active in the current struggle to counterattack
the Right deviationist wind to reverse the ver-
dicts of the cultural revolution stirred up by
Teng Hsiao-ping, unrepentant capitalist-roader
in the Party. With proletarian indignation and
citing achievements in their own factory, they
criticize Teng Hsiao-ping's servile philosophy
of developing industry by becoming dependent
on importing foreign technology and equipment.
They are firm in keeping on the road of self-
reliance and maintaining the initiative in
industrialization as urged by Chairman Mao.[10]

From personal experience, this writer can attest to
the fact that the cases just cited are reflected in Chinese
attitudes toward proposals from American business firms. By
nature pragmatic and impatient, U.S. exporters have argued
with the Chinese that self-reliance carried too far will
uselessly squander the time of designers, engineers, and
workers. Importers have told the Chinese that trial-by
error methods to produce for the large U.S. market--in-
sistence upon creating a demand for Chinese-designed products bearing Chinese brand names--will likewise waste
time and money. More than once, in discussions like this,
I have heard a Chinese negotiator tell the following
story, one of Chairman Mao's favorites:

There is an ancient Chinese fable called "The
Foolish Old Man Who Removed the Mountains." It
tells of an old man who lived in northern China
long, long ago and was known as the Foolish Old
Man of North Mountain. His house faced south
and beyond his doorway stood the two great peaks,
Taihang and Wangwu, obstructing the way. With
great determination, he led his sons in digging
up these mountains hoe in hand. Another greybeard,
known as the Wise Old Man, saw them and said
derisively, "How silly of you to do this! It is
quite impossible for you few to dig up these
two huge mountains." The Foolish Old Man replied,
"When I die, my sons will carry on; when they
die, there will be my grandsons, and then their
sons and grandsons, and so on to infinity. High
as they are, the mountains cannot grow any higher
and with every bit we dig, they will be that much
lower. Why can't we clear them away?" Having
refuted the Wise Old Man's wrong view, he went
on digging every day, unshaken in his convic-
tion.[11]

In assessing Chinese trade principles in the aftermath
of the anti-Teng campaign and in the midst of the anti-"Gang
of Four" campaign, one is driven to the conclusion that

Robert Scalapino is right when he says that the fate of Mao
may resemble the fate of Confucius--that of continuous rein-
terpretation depending on the needs and ambitions of those
who follow.

China's Foreign Trade Apparatus

Most foreign countries offer the foreign businessman a
commercial environment hospitable to direct and indirect
investment in a variety of forms. The most populous nation
on earth does not. A recent issue of Peking Review, in fact,
reminded readers, "Marx pointed out that swindling is one
of the characteristics of capitalist commerce,"12 and thus
while business is being done with the West, it is transacted
in a setting unfamiliar to many U.S. firms.

In China it is impossible for foreign firms to lease a
local office or hire a single local employee, much less to
form a local partnership or corporation or establish a local
plant. It is not possible to buy any local real or intangi-
ble property. It is not possible to make a capital investment of even one cent in any local enterprise or to form a
joint venture with any local entity. It is not even possible to travel to China to discuss the sale of plant equipment or technology without a firm prior invitation in
writing. Nor, of course, can any enterprising Chinese
start a business of his own in China.

To look at this another way, it is as if all business
in the United States, from the Good Humor Man to Exxon, were
suddenly conducted entirely by the U.S. government, and the
Commerce Department conducted all foreign transactions for
every factory or user in the country.

Foreign trade in China is a monopoly of the state, and
is conducted principally through eight Foreign Trade Corporations (FTCs). Neither manufacturing nor production
units in China, nor Chinese end-user entities, conclude
contracts with foreign individuals or firms; instead, the
FTCs act as their agents.

The FTCs carry out a trade plan under the guidance of
the Ministry of Foreign Trade, aided in part by the China
Council for the Promotion of International Trade (CCPIT).
In addition to headquarters at Peking, the Foreign Trade
Ministry maintains local bureaus in major Chinese cities,
and the FTCs and the CCPIT also have local branches and
offices in certain cities.

The Ministry of Foreign Trade

Under the supervision of the Staff Office of Finance and
Trade of China's State Council, the Ministry of Foreign

Trade formulates an overall import and export plan to be used as a basis for specific planning by the FTCs and other agencies with collateral foreign trade responsibilities. After review and approval by the Trade Ministry of their specific import-export plans, the FTCs carry out, under ministry supervision, their individual trade plans.

Only through a minute analysis of China's actual sales and purchases, which are kept secret, can the broad outlines of these plans be perceived. A foreign firm seeking to determine the business possible in its line must thus accumulate and assess the foreign trade data published by China's trading partners--not an easy task, and not one that yields complete information.

In the absence of other kinds of information, businessmen are wise to heed occasional general statements emanating from China which not only embody current trade principles but despite deliberate ambiguity do illuminate the factors at work influencing the trade policymakers. An article by Foreign Trade Minister Li Chiang appearing in the periodical China's Foreign Trade, for example, reminds readers that in pursuing international trade China seeks "to learn from other countries' merits and obtain necessary materials, equipment and techniques through exchange."[13]

The Ministry of Foreign Trade is organized into eight bureaus. Of these, five have geographic responsibility, while the others handle import, export, and planning matters. In addition to administrative offices, the ministry oversees customs, commodities inspection of imports and exports, a training school for foreign trade personnel, and a market study institute, as well as eight FTCs, a ship-chartering corporation, and a national transportation corporation.

China's Foreign Trade Corporations

The actual conduct of China's foreign trade rests with China's Foreign Trade Corporations. These FTCs at present number eight, seven of which have both import and export jurisdiction.[14] Only the China National Technical Import Corporation (Techimport) concerns itself solely with imports into China, and its areas of interest are complete plants and advanced technology.

The corporate charters of the FTCs, if any, have never been made public. The legal nature of the existence of the FTCs is therefore unclear. What is clear is that the FTCs act as the exclusive agents for China's producing and consuming entities in the sale and purchase of goods with foreign firms. Presumably the FTCs do have some "profit and loss" accountability. Whether they are "legal persons" capable of suing or being sued is a somewhat moot

point: there are no civil courts as such in China and the
FTCs maintain no offices or assets abroad.   They do act on
occasion through "agents" abroad, which are probably more
accurately considered independent contractors.
    Contracts concluded with foreign firms usually do not
bear the name of the Chinese end-users seeking foreign goods
or equipment.   Instead, the name of the FTC concerned, or
its municipal or regional branch, appears as the Chinese
party to the agreement.   It is the staff of the FTC, supplemented only when and as necessary by knowledgeable producers,
end-users, or technicians, which carries on negotiations
with foreign firms and executes contracts.
    The Chinese Export Commodities Fair, China's principal
export event, is organized and operated by the FTCs, and it
is at this biannual fair that the FTCs are seen functioning
in the fashion intended for them.   FTC representatives from
Peking, augmented by negotiators from the regional and municipal branches, come to Kwangchow (Canton) each spring and
fall to sit across the table from foreign traders and negotiate all terms and conditions of purchases and sales.
    When purchasing from abroad, the FTCs seek not only to
achieve the best terms for a given item or technology but
also make an effort to ferret out from the supplier or
licenser information on the nature and price of competitive
products and processes.
    As would seem obvious, the FTCs are functionally
organized first into import departments and then sub-
divided into units, each with responsibility for certain
of the many products handled by the corporation as a whole.
In addition, within these divisions are geographically
composed departments, so that expertise can be developed
and maintained with respect to the peculiarities of
different foreign countries and areas.

                Collateral Trade and Related Organizations

In addition to the FTCs, there are other agencies which do
not handle the purchase or sale of merchandise but which are
nevertheless an integral part of the foreign trade apparatus.
These include:
    China National Foreign Trade Transportation Corporation,
which arranges documentation, shipping, and delivery of
imported and export goods.
    China National Chartering Corporation, which charters
vessels and books shipping space for Chinese cargoes.
    China Commodities Inspection Bureau, which performs
final inspection of imported and export goods on behalf of
the FTCs to determine whether or not such goods are in
conformity with underlying contracts.
    Bank of China, which from its head office in Peking and

branches abroad handles all foreign exchanges transactions for China, including international payments and disbursements as required by China's foreign trade corporations.

People's Insurance Company of China, which underwrites marine, land transportation, air transportation, post, ship's hull, and machinery insurance and reinsurance.

China Insurance Company Ltd., a joint state-private enterprise, which underwrites marine, fire, life, accident, workmen's compensation, and motor vehicle insurance.

The Tai Ping Insurance Company Ltd., another state-private enterprise, whose business parallels that of the China Insurance Company.

China National Export Commodities Packaging Corporation, created in 1974, which, among others functions, advises the FTCs on packing and packaging requirements of foreign markets.

China Publications Center (Guozi Shudian), which handles books, periodicals, phonograph records, and postcards and functions in particular as the export agent for China's publications in foreign languages.

China Film Distribution and Exhibition Corporation, which is the sole importer of foreign films and the export agent for Chinese films.

China Stamp Export Company, which is the exclusive agent for the export of Chinese stamps.

Chinese Scientific and Technical Association, which is involved, with the CCPIT, in arranging contacts between China's scientific and technical communities and professional societies and associations abroad.

All of the foregoing agencies are based in Peking and, with the exception of the Packaging Corporation, have branch offices in a number of other Chinese cities. All are likewise represented at the Chinese Export Commodities Fair.

The China Council for the Promotion of International Trade

Aiding the Ministry of Trade and the FTCs is an organization known as the China Council for the Promotion of International Trade (CCPIT). The CCPIT, founded in 1952, is described in China's publications as "a permanent agency performing duties similar to those of Chambers of International Commerce in other countries." It has been described by its leadership to this writer as "a people-to-people organization, not a governmental organization." Without its own sources of income, however, it can only be financed through an appropriation by the Chinese government. Whatever its charter, which remains secret, it seems clear that the CCPIT is governed today by persons from the eight FTCs, the Ministry of Foreign Trade, and the Ministry of Foreign Affairs, who, acting as a kind of board of directors,

meet periodically to review and formulate plans and
activities.
    A permanent staff, supervised by a chairman, several
vice-chairmen, a secretary-general, and a deputy secretary-
general, consists of six major departments in addition to
units responsible for administration and research. These
are:
    Legal Affairs Department, which advised the CCPIT's
Foreign Trade Arbitration Commission and Maritime Arbitration
Commission; informs the FTCs and other trade agencies about
trade-related legal developments and requirements abroad;
analyzes foreign contracts, laws, and regulations having an
impact on China's trade; and oversees registration of foreign
trademarks.
    Department for Average Adjustment, which administers
the Provisional Rules for General Average Adjustment promul-
gated by the CCPIT.
    Liaison Department, which sends and receives foreign
trade delegations and maintains contact with trade associations in other countries.
    Foreign Exhibitions in China Department, which assists
foreign countries, associations, and companies in staging
trade exhibitions and technical symposia in China.
    Overseas Exhibitions Department, which is responsible
for organizing China's trade exhibitions abroad.
    Publicity Department, which publishes a variety of
periodicals describing China's economy and foreign trade.
    Despite the independent status claimed for it, it can
be safely assumed that no significant activity is undertaken by the CCPIT without the prior approval or direction
of the Chinese government as expressed through the relevant
ministries. This is to be expected in part because it is
the CCPIT which is the main commercial link to countries,
like the United States, which do not enjoy diplomatic
relations with China. Indeed, the CCPIT has in the past
signed, in its own name, trade accords of commercial consequence with foreign trading firms or trade associations
semigovernmental or private in character. The CCPIT also
plays some part in the organization and conduct of the
twice-yearly Chinese Export Commodities Fair at Kwangchow
(Canton).

The Chinese Export Commodities Fair

In the annals of international trade, it would probably be
impossible to find a foreign commercial event which has
exerted so magnetic a pull over so great a distance on so
many American businessmen as the Chinese Export Commodities
Fair, more often referred to as the Canton or Kwangchow
Fair.

The fair has been held twice each year, in the spring between April 15 and May 15 and in the autumn between October 15 and November 15, at Kwangchow (Canton) since 1957. Attendance is by invitation only. Americans were not invited until April 1972, the first fair following the visit to China by President Nixon in February of that year.

It is estimated by some that, since the 1972 spring Fair, no fewer than 75,000 U.S. businessmen have sought-- unsuccessfully--to gain admission to the fair. Probably not more than 2 percent of that number have actually attended to date. Yet, enthusiasm has not dimmed, and requests for invitations to forthcoming fairs are still flowing to Peking.

How Peking Views the Fair

The most authoritative, if brief, explanation of the fair is provided by the Chinese in a pocket handbook provided free to fairgoers as they register for the event. It says that the fair is "jointly sponsored by China's import and export corporations in accordance with the directive of the great leader of the Chinese people, Chairman Mao," once again citing the justification for contact with foreign traders, that "the Chinese people wish to have friendly cooperation with the people of all countries and to resume and expand international trade in order to develop production and promote economic prosperity."

"The Fair," says the handbook "takes the form of com- bining trade negotiations with the display of exhibits." The FTCs are represented at the fair by trading delega- tions, and "on-the-spot business talks are held and trans- actions against samples concluded between the trading delegations and businessmen from all parts of the world." At the fair, where Peking does between 35 and 40 percent of its export business annually, "China sells her export commodities and buys what she needs, while views are exchanged for the development of reciprocal trade."

The fair is not without political content:

> Introduced in each Hall are some of the outstanding deeds performed by the Chinese people as a result of studying and applying Marxism-Leninism-Mao Tsetung Thought in grasping revolution and promoting produc- tion. Put on display are a rich and varied range of export commodities and products of successful achieve- ments from China's various provinces, municipalities, and autonomous regions (with the exception of Taiwan Province), reflecting the new attainments in socialist revolution and construction scored by the Chinese people under the guidance of Chairman Mao's prole- tarian revolutionary line.

> Fairgoers are reminded:

Following the daily development of China's socialist
construction and the constant development of her foreign relations, the scope of the Fair has continuously
expanded. The number of foreign guests visiting the
Fair has increased from 1,200 from over 20 countries
and regions at the first session of the Fair to more
than 26,000 from over 100 countries and regions....
The volume of both import and export trade has also
increased with each passing year. Since its inaugura-
tion, by resolutely carrying out China's foreign trade
policy of "equality, mutual benefit and supplying each
other's needs," the Fair has promoted normal trade
exchange between China and the rest of the world and
enhanced mutual understanding and friendship between
the Chinese people and the peoples of all countries.
Though the Fair is, as its name suggests, an event
designed to sell China's goods and thus earn foreign
exchange, it is not an ordinary "profit-motivated"
event, as a number of characteristics of the Fair
clearly reveal.
Businessmen are put on notice of the political
character of the Fair, and of some Fair business
decisions, by a quotation from Mao Tsetung displayed
on a large red billboard which, together with a portrait of Chairman Mao, dominates the entrance lobby
of the main Fair exhibition hall: "The Theoretical
Basis Guiding Our Thinking Is Marxism-Leninism."

The New China News Agency dispatch announcing the opening of the spring 1975 Fair led with this paragraph, another
of many indicators that business is not alone the substance
of the Fair: "China's Export Commodities Fair opened here
today as the nationwide movement to criticize Lin Piao and
Confucius is deepening and advancing victoriously."

By April 1976 this kind of criticism was being directed
to the "arch unrepentant capitalist-roader" Teng Hsiao-
p'ing, and slogans attacking him were evident throughout
the Fair.

On opening day, red balloons trailed inscribed streamers over the fairgrounds, but the messages were political,
not commercial. Among them: "Resolutely support the just
demands of the Third World!", "Long live the victory of
the Great Proletarian Cultural Revolution!", and "Long
live Marxism-Leninism-Mao Tse-tung Thought!"

At the banquet which closed the fair, officials
summarized the event by announcing that China "will adhere
to the principle of independence, initiative and self-
reliance, grasp revolution, promote production, and expand
our foreign trade on the basis of developing industry
and agriculture in a big way, so as to serve China's
socialist construction better and contribute to the
promotion of friendship between the Chinese people and

the people of other countries."

Organization of the Fair

Kwangchow (Canton) today is China's principal trading center, as it has always been so far as Western traders are concerned. Though the historic city has over time permitted the introduction of foreign goods into China, it has principally been an outlet for Chinese merchandise. And it is so today.

Recent American visitors to the fair have discovered, as their forebearers did, that their travel in China is essentially confined to Canton. John Paton Davies, writing of another era, says that: "China humored the seaborne barbarians to the extent of tolerating foreign merchants at one port only, Canton. It was the tradesman's entrance, where they were treated as disreputable peddlers, not permitted to cross the threshold into the house." Today foreign businessmen, with a few exceptions, are likewise allowed no further than Canton. Each fair finds a large number of them, especially Americans, dickering with the Chinese for permission to leave sweltering Canton for sightseeing in Peking or Shanghai. But the fair is not intended as a tourist attraction. Political overtones notwithstanding, the main emphasis is on selling. And the Chinese have done a great deal to make the businessmen's sojourn in Canton as pleasant as possible.

The Chinese obviously intend to maintain and expand Canton as the prime trading city of the People's Republic. Beginning with the spring 1974 Fair, the event was moved to an enormous modern complex of buildings, newly constructed, with over a million square feet of display area and negotiating rooms at the northern end of the city. At the same fair, the Chinese opened an 800-room, 11-story addition to the Tung Fang Hotel, across the street from the fair compound, and inaugurated a massive new railroad station which now deposits visitors within a 15-minute walk of the fair buildings, the Tung Fang Hotel, and two beautiful public parks boasting lakes, boating, swimming, restaurants, and other facilities. The Tung Fang Hotel, in a move almost unthinkable in austere China, now offers an artificial pond with lounge chairs arranged in a secluded garden around it, two bars, a billiard room, a table-tennis room, a badminton court, a barber shop, a beauty parlor, a shopping arcade, and a roof garden for the convenience of fair guests. Business is made easier with the recent introduction at the hotel of telex as well as cable, overseas telephone, banking, and postal facilities.

Display areas in the fair complex, arranged by the foreign trade corporations, beautifully exhibit thousands of varieties of merchandise, from numerically controlled machine tools to frozen foods, from petroleum products

to textiles and handicrafts. Access to the fairgrounds
is strictly limited to registered businessmen, identifi-
able by a pink ribbon bearing the Chinese characters for
"Honored Guest."

In addition to the exhibit of goods available for
export, numerous displays, consisting of large photographs
and massive topographic scale models, show the visitor
examples of rural or industrial achievements. Such displays are ordinarily manned by very personable young men
and women guides from the area represented in the exhibit.
In other areas, workers demonstrate the skills which
have made Chinese art objects and handicrafts among the
finest in the world.

Weekend excursions are arranged for groups of fairgoers to visit model factories, communes, schools, hospitals, power stations, and the like. Travel without escort
for shopping or sightseeing may be undertaken throughout
the city of Canton, without restriction, but special permission must be obtained to go beyond the city limits.
So complete are the services and amenities available within
walking distance of the fair, however, that many guests
never venture into the city proper.

The business aids available at the Tung Fang Hotel
(and other major hotels in the city used by fairgoers) are
also available at the fair compound itself. Telex, cable,
overseas telephone, typewriters, banking, post office,
insurance, shipping, and customs services are all provided
for the foreign trader. A cinema, garden, restaurant,
and retail stores round out the amenities at the fairgrounds.

Actual business at the fair is transacted mostly in
private discussion rooms on floors above the exhibit
areas, though owing to lack of space even in this large
complex some contract negotiation occurs at tables in display areas essentially without privacy and occasionally
in the presence of competing business representatives.

A permanent secretariat based in Canton throughout
the year conducts logistic planning between fairs and
carries on the day-to-day business of fair organization
and operation. Opening and closing days of the fair are
marked with ear-shattering fireworks displays, specially
lighted streets and buildings, and mass banquets, the
largest of which is held at the Tung Fang Hotel where
several thousand guests are addressed, usually by a vice-
minister of foreign trade. Throughout the fair, Canton's
restaurants and other public places are bedecked with
signs or streamers extending "Warm Welcome to the Guests
of the Chinese Export Commodities Fair." Students from
China's foreign language institutes appear in the city,
where the best of them are utilized as interpreters in
business discussions and those with less experience are

employed as hotel and restaurant workers.

The fair, then, serves primarily as China's sales outlet to the world. Secondarily, it is a showcase of socialist achievement, not only to the West and to the Third World, but also to China's own citizens who may occasionally be seen in special groups moving through the complex. Finally, the fair localizes commercial activity with foreigners as to time and place, and permits a relatively orderly conduct of trade.

Other Chinese Trade Fairs

In a departure from earlier practice, in which the Chinese Export Commodities Fair alone was the mechanism for export sales, the China National Native Produce and Animal By-Products Import and Export Corporation held two new sales events beginning early 1975. Between February and early March, Carpet Fairs have been held at Tientsin, and a Forestal Products Fair has been held at Kwangchow. The goods displayed and sold at these events are no different from those ordinarily handled at the Canton Fair, and it now appears that these and similar such events--handling straw goods, handicrafts, textiles, and the like--will become regular annual events.

China's Foreign Trade Performance

The following tables are useful guides in assessing the performance of China's foreign trade.

China's Foreign Trade (in $ billions)

Year	Imports	Exports	Total
1975	7.3	6.9	14.3
1974	7.3	6.5	13.9
1973	4.98	4.90	9.88
1972	2.84	3.08	5.92
1971	2.31	2.41	4.72
1970	2.24	2.05	4.29
1969	1.83	2.03	3.86
1968	1.82	1.94	3.76
1967	1.95	1.95	3.90
1966	2.03	2.21	4.24
1965	1.84	2.04	3.88
1964	1.47	1.75	3.22
1963	1.20	1.57	2.77
1962	1.15	1.53	2.68
1961	1.49	1.53	3.02
1960	2.03	1.96	3.99
1952	1.01	.88	1.89

U.S.-China Trade (in $ millions)

Year	U.S. exports	U.S. imports	Total	Approximate ratio
1971	-0-	4.9	4.9	--
1972	63.5	32.4	95.9	2:1
1973	739.7a	63.9	803.6	12:1
1974	820.5b	114.7	935.2	7:1
1975	303.6	170.9	474.5	2:1
	122.0	106.0	--	--
1976c	100.0	200.0	350.0	1:2

     a.   Includes $50.6 million of U.S. cotton transhipped through Canada.
     b.   Includes $11.7 million of U.S. soybeans transhipped through Canada.
     c.   Estimate.

Major Commodities in U.S. Trade with the People's Republic of China

	Commodity	Exports (millions of U.S. $)			
		Total 1974	Total 1975	Jan.-Mar. 1975	Jan.-Mar. 1976
0	Food and live animals	329.70	0.02	0.00	0.00
1	Beverages and tobacco	2.72	0.00	0.00	Z
2	Crude materials, inedible, except fuels	328.08	100.13	26.81	7.35
3	Mineral fuels, lubricants, and related products	0.23	0.20	0.11	0.02
4	Animal and vege-table oils and fats	7.54	0.01	0.00	0.00
5	Chemicals	10.18	5.28	1.67	4.02
6	Manufactured goods by chief materials	18.59	73.75	5.96	35.24
7	Machinery and transport equip-ment	106.75	118.80	34.75	37.62
8	Misc. manufactured articles NES	2.71	4.97	0.90	1.16
9	Items and trans n/class	0.35	0.47	0.00	Z
	Total	806.85	303.63	70.21	85.42

Major Commodities in U.S. Trade with the People's Republic of China (cont.)

General imports (millions of U.S. $)

	Commodity	Total 1974	Total 1975	Jan.-Mar. 1975	Jan.-Mar. 1976
0	Food and live animals	13.45	15.66	2.88	6.27
1	Beverages and tobacco	2.83	2.56	0.29	0.21
2	Crude materials, inedible, except fuels	16.33	19.25	4.89	7.67
3	Mineral fuels, lubricants, and related products	0.11	0.00	0.00	0.00
4	Animal and vegetable oils and fats	0.37	1.91	1.02	1.01
5	Chemicals	18.36	15.92	5.46	3.01
6	Manufactured goods by chief materials	42.74	88.58	17.32	18.25
7	Machinery and transport equipment	0.09	0.30	0.04	0.08
8	Misc. manufactured articles NES	19.23	25.29	5.70	11.88
9	Items and trans n/class	1.16	1.50	0.48	0.65
	Total	114.68	170.96	38.07	49.03

Source: National Council for U.S.-China Trade, Sept. 1976.

Comparative Trade Statistics

1. Total trade, 1975

U.S.A.	R.O.C.	P.R.C.	NICARAGUA
$211.06 billion	$11.2 billion	$14.3 billion	$892 million
(imports--$107.65) (exports--$103.41)	(imports--$5.9 billion) (exports--$5.3 billion)	(imports--$6.9 billion) (exports--$7.3 billion)	

2. Trade with U.S., 1975

R.O.C.		P.R.C.		NICARAGUA	
U.S. imp.	U.S. exp.	U.S. imp.	U.S. exp.	U.S. imp.	U.S. exp.
$1.66 billion	$1.00 billion	$303.6 million	$170.9 million	$131 million	$156 million
Total		Total		Total	
$3.4 billion		$474.5 million		$287 million	

3. Trade forecasts, 1976

U.S.-R.O.C. total trade $4.50 billion

U.S.-P.R.C. total trade $300.0 million (less than one tenth of R.O.C. trade)

4. If P.R.C.'s foreign trade was as great, per capita, as that of the R.O.C., its total trade would be $448 billion or more than double that of the United States!

Notes

1. Analects.
2. Chou Hua-min, addressing the UNCTAD Conference in Santiago, Chile, 1972.
3. There are important subsidiary trade principles. These are not as widely expressed as those discussed in the text, but they are just as surely followed. In summary form they are:
    1. China will not go into debt in order to finance imports; i.e., China is not interested in long-term foreign financing.
    2. China will import only what is essential for socialist construction, i.e., no consumer goods, luxury items, or goods which can be made in China.
    3. China will finance imports as much as possible through exports and will try to balance trade bilaterally where possible.
4. China's Foreign Trade, no. 1 (1974): 3.
5. A Glance at China's Economy (Peking: Foreign Language Press, 1974), p. 41.
6. Quotations from Chairman Mao Tsetung (2d ed., Peking: Foreign Language Press, 1974), p. 194.
7. Li Chiang, in China's Foreign Trade, no. 1(1974): 4.
8. Ibid., p. 4.
9. Quoted from a reprint of the article "Gang of Four Sabotages Foreign Trade" appearing in Ta-kung pao [L'Impartial] (Hong Kong), Jan. 20, 1977, p. 6.
10. China Reconstructs, Sept. 1976, pp. 34-35.
11. As recorded in Quotations from Chairman Mao Tsetung, p. 201.
12. Peking Review 18, no. 24 (June 13, 1975): 27.
13. China's Foreign Trade, no. 1 (1974): 5.
14. The Foreign Trade Corporations are constituted on a product basis, as follows: (1) China National Cereals, Oils, and Foodstuffs Import and Export Corporation; (2) China National Native Produce and Animal By-Products Import and Export Corporation; (3) China National Textiles Import and Export Corporation; (4) China National Light Industrial Products Import and Export Corporation; (5) China National Chemicals Import and Export Corporation; (6) China National Machinery Import and Export Corporation; (7) China National Metals and Minerals Import and Export Corporation; and (8) China National Technical Import Corporation.
    It is an arresting coincidence of history that China's trade in the late eighteenth century was likewise monopolized, then by eight Chinese merchant firms operating with the imperial sanction of the Dragon Throne at Peking. There ends, however, the resemblance with the past.

4. U.S.-China Trade: An Appraisal

Robert F. Dernberger

The institutional and political framework of the U.S.-
China trade and an analysis of China's overall trade are
fully covered in other chapters. Thus, I will restrict
my essay to an analysis of the particular statistical
results and future prospects in the bilateral trade between these two countries--one the largest economy in
the world in terms of GNP, the other the largest in terms
of people (and seventh largest in terms of GNP). Yet, the
trade between these two countries at its peak in 1974 was
less than 0.05 of a percent of total world trade and less
than 1 percent of the total trade of the United States.
Most people probably are familiar with the general arguments as to why this bilateral trade is so small, arguments involving the size of China's internal market, the
postwar political and military hostilities between the
United States and China, the antitrade biases in China's
economic institutions and economic policies, and the
simple, yet basic arguments concerning the complementarity,
or lack of it, between China's export supplies and the
United States' demands. My purpose will not be to review
these factors, which obviously explain, in large part,
the evolution of U.S.-China trade since 1971. Rather, I
want to interpret the empirical evidence of the trade
which has taken place in the past five years as a guide
to the future prospects for U.S.-China trade.
     Some readers may remember my earlier attempt to spell
out the prospects for trade between the United States and
China, an attempt made in 1969, at a time when there had
been no evidence of trade between these countries since
the early 1950s. I am referring to my paper, "Prospects
for Trade between China and the United States," published
in China Trade Prospects and U.S. Policy," edited by
Alexander Eckstein and published by Praeger for the
National Committee on United States-China Relations in
1971. At the time when that study was made, a commonly
heard argument against opening trade with China was the
existence, then, of a serious balance of payments problem for the United States; it was feared the opening of
trade with China would expose our domestic market to cheap
labor imports, making our balance of payments problem
even worse. My study was an attempt to determine if
those arguments had any validity.
     I will not bore the reader with the details or
mechanics of my estimates, but I simply cannot ignore
this opportunity to stick up for them, seven years later,
now that we have some empirical evidence to test them.
Let me quote the results: "this writer believes that,

of all the estimates presented in Table 10, the most
plausible are those depicting a balanced trade of $25
million each way (a 'pessimistic' estimate), or U.S.
imports of $200 million and exports of $325 million (an
'optimistic' estimate)."[1] These were estimates for the
possible level of China-U.S. trade in 1980. It must be
pointed out these estimates were made in 1969, in terms
of prices prevailing in 1969. Thus, given the average
annual rate of price increases, these estimates should
be revised upward by about 100 percent (i.e., doubled)
to be expressed in terms of "expected" current prices in
1980. In current prices, therefore, my estimates for
1980 become $50 million each way, $400 million each way,
or U.S. imports of $400 and exports of $650 million.

      In examining the evidence of the past five years
(see Table 1), I begin with U.S. imports because they are
the easiest to explain: In million current U.S. dollars
they were 5 in 1971, 32 in 1972, 65 in 1973, 115 in 1974,
and 158 in 1975. If these admittedly limited number of

Table 1. U.S.-China Trade, 1971-75

A. U.S. exports to China (million current U.S. dollars)

	1971	1972	1973	1974	1975
Total	0	64	740	819	304
Commodity composition (in %)					
Wheat			40.3	28.5	--
Cotton			14.6	22.7	26.2
Soybeans			6.3	17.1	--
Soybean oil			2.6	--	--
Corn			19.2	11.4	--
Aluminum			--	--	15.4
Aircraft			8.5	2.0	--
Machinery			--	--	7.3
Gas compressors			--	--	4.5
Steam engines and turbines			--	--	4.1
Scrap metal			3.5	1.1	2.7
Fabricated iron and steel			--	--	2.1
Fertilizer			0.7	--	--
Tallow			--	0.9	--
Telecommunications equipment			0.6	--	--
Other			3.7	12.0	37.7

Table 1. (cont.)

B. U.S. imports from China (million current U.S. dollars)

	1971	1972	1973	1974	1975
Total	5	32	65	115	158
Commodity composition (in %)					
Tin			12.2	8.2	25.6
Cotton Textiles			9.5	15.9	17.3
Antiques			8.8	5.9	2.8
Bristles			11.2	5.2	2.2
Rosin			2.4	6.9	2.6
Silk			6.8	2.2	2.2
Fireworks			5.0	--	1.8
Brooms, brushes, dusters			3.1	--	--
Animals hairs			2.2	--	--
Shrimps			--	4.6	--
Cigarettes			--	2.2	--
Woven baskets and bags			--	--	1.6
Other			36.4	48.9	43.9

Source: Data are taken from various issues of U.S.-China
Business Review.
Note: It is very important to note that the commodity
composition percentages are based on data for the ten leading exports and imports in each year, according to the
seven-digit commodity classification used by the U.S.
Department of Commerce. Thus, for example, the entry for
cotton textile exports from China to the United States includes only those exports in each seven-digit classification within cotton textiles which were large enough to
rank among China's top ten commodity exports to the United
States in each year; other cotton textile exports to the
United States which were smaller than about 1 or 2 percent of total Chinese exports to the United States are
included in "Other."

observations for the past five years are used to forecast
a trend over the next five years, China's exports to the
United States in 1980 would be 350 million current U.S.
dollars, i.e., within the bounds of both the neutral and
optimistic estimates made several years ago.[2]
    In support of this forecasted growth trend in Chinese
exports to the United States is the tremendous diversification, except for textiles and tin, in the commodity composition of these exports, i.e., sudden swings in the export
of any particular commodity or group of commodities to the
United States is not likely to lead to a sudden swing in
the level of total Chinese exports to the United States.

At the single-digit commodity classification level, manufactured goods (category 6) accounted for one-third and
one-half of China's exports to the United States in 1974
and 1975, respectively. The dominance of this export
category is entirely explained by the fact that China's
two largest individual commodity exports to the United
States are within this same single-digit category:
cotton woven fabrics and tin and tin alloys. Cotton
fabrics accounted for 21 percent of China's exports to
the United States in 1974, 18 percent of the total in
1975; tin accounted for 8 percent of China's exports to
the United States in 1974, 25 percent in 1975. At the
one-digit commodity classification level, no other commodity category accounted for more than 20 percent of
total Chinese exports to the United States in 1974 and
1975, and the next largest category, after manufactured
goods, was manufactured goods, not specified. At the
four-digit level, again after cotton fabrics and tin,
which together accounted for one-third and one-half of
the total, no other individual commodity category accounted for more than 7 percent in 1974 or 4 percent in 1975
of China's exports to the United States, and these third
largest exports were residual categories: wood- and resin-
based chemical products, n.e.s. (1974) and materials of
animal origin, n.e.s. (1975). With the exception of cotton
fabrics and tin, therefore, the explanation of China's
exports to the United States over the past five years is
to be found in a wide variety of export commodity categories. Inasmuch as this expected diversification was
built into our earlier projections, including the expected
relative dominance of cotton fabrics and tin, and there
would appear to be no indication of any threat of instability in this trend at the present time, I see no
reason for rejecting my earlier projections of Chinese
exports to the United States growing to a level of
approximately 400 million U.S. dollars by 1980.

        I do, however, see two major objections which may be
raised against my simple extrapolation of the past into
the future: the possibility of the United States granting
most-favored-nation tariff treatment to China and the
possibility of Chinese petroleum exports to the United
States. Both these topics are discussed more fully in
other papers and I merely will offer my own opinions very
briefly at this point. As far as the importance of the
most-favored-nation (MFN) tariff, the relatively slow
growth of Chinese exports to the United States over the
past five years is believed by some observers to be due
to Chinese exports--in the absence of MFN tariffs--being
taxed at the relatively high rates of the 1930 Smoot-
Hawley tariff schedule.[3]

        The granting of MFN tariff treatment to China is one

of the possible concessions available to the United States
in our present political negotiations with the Chinese.
It is viewed as a concession, because it is believed that,
if granted to China, this would give the Chinese greater
access to our internal markets, resulting in a significant
increase in Chinese exports to the United States. This
step in logic, however, only follows if the Chinese react
by maintaining present Chinese delivery prices on their
exports so that the U.S. domestic price is lowered by the
amount of the decline in the effective tariff, the price
elasticity of demand for China's exports is very high, and
the Chinese elasticity of export supply to the United States
is very high. I do not believe any of these conditions
would hold true; past Chinese price behavior indicates
they would take advantage of the lower tariffs to raise
the prices they receive, while lowering the price paid
by the U.S. end-user, with the U.S. tax collector absorb-
ing the loss; the U.S. demand for the goods most affected
is not large to begin with, whether price elastic or not;
and China would be able to meet increased demands in the
U.S. market most easily by diverting exports from other
import markets rather than by increasing their total supply, given the excess demand already existing in the
Chinese domestic market. Finally, the possibility, which
is sometimes mentioned, that the Chinese would reallocate
investment so as to take advantage of the lower tariffs
on U.S. imports ignores the already high priority claims
on those investment funds within China's development
program and--for that matter--the basic long-run goal
of self-reliance which underlies China's development
program. Textiles, one of China's two largest exports
to the United States, is an exception to the above argument, but the quantity of our textile imports is controlled directly and not by tariff adjustments. In short,
I believe the MFN tariff is a marginal issue in forecasting the future for China's exports to the United States,
although I readily admit it is an important political
issue between these two countries at the present time.
     As for potential Chinese oil exports to the United
States, I am equally pessimistic. The U.S. imports of
petroleum products from China were worth only $110,000
in 1974 and zero in 1975. There is no doubt, however,
that Chinese petroleum output will continue to grow rapidly
in the foreseeable future. Yet, these developments probably will have a much greater impact on U.S. exports to
China, i.e., exports of petroleum extraction and refining
equipment, than on China's exports to the United States.
Here I can only refer to the conclusions of a U.S. government agency's rather mechanical projection, but one which
is strongly supported by a much more sophisticated estimate
by Kim Woodard at Stanford:[4] given reasonable expectations

of China's domestic economic development and production of
energy sources, along with allowance for a rational, and
even necessary, substitution of petroleum for coal and
electricity as a source of energy, domestic demand will
absorb most of China's energy supplies, leaving <u>relatively</u>
small amounts for export. Moreover, most of this <u>potential</u>
surplus undoubtedly will go to other countries in Asia.

So much for potential Chinese exports to the United
States. I now turn to the Chinese import side of this
bilateral trade, which is much more difficult to predict.
In 1969 few seriously argued with my estimates of potential
U.S. exports to China; the arguments were mainly on the
Chinese export side. Yet, within a few years after Sino-
American trade began, I was proved wrong and my error was
in my projections of U.S. exports, not imports. United
States exports to China in current million U.S. dollars
were 0 in 1971, 64 in 1972, 740 in 1973, 819 in 1974, and
304 in 1975. As the level of these exports approached the
billion mark in 1974, I took my lumps as a forecaster and
was told, secondhand, that the secretary of state of the
United States, justifiably boasting about the fruits of his
foreign policy initiatives, argued the benefits of Sino-
American trade ties already realized had proved the pessimistic expectations of the academic experts wrong in only
three short years.

Thanks to the decline in Chinese imports from the
United States in 1975, the empirical evidence of the past
five years indicates a trend which would yield a level of
Chinese imports from the United States in 1980 of only
1,340 million current U.S. dollars in 1980; only three
times my "neutral" projection and more than double my
"optimistic" projection.[5] Although the decline in Chinese
imports from the United States in 1975 means this mathe-
matical extrapolation of past trends makes my projections
look a little better than the development in 1971-74 did,
even if actual developments through the remainder of the
1970s were to vindicate my projections, my forecast for
Chinese imports from the United States are wrong. They
are wrong for a simple reason: my estimates of China's
future demand for imports were based on estimates of the
demand for machinery and equipment and metal products
generated by the needs of China's continued industrialization; they did not include any consideration of China's
potential demand for foodstuffs due to their continued
inability to solve their agricultural problems.

To show clearly the unstable, and somewhat unpredictable, impact of China's agricultural problem on China's
imports from the United States over the past five years,
we can separate those imports into agricultural and nonagricultural products. In the nonagricultural category
(mostly machinery), China's imports from the United States,

in current million U.S. dollars, were 0 in 1971, 2 in 1972,
92 in 1973, 164 in 1974, and 225 in 1975. The time trend
in these exports over the past five years is very stable,
with a coefficient of correlation of 0.98, and projects a
level of Chinese imports of nonagricultural goods from the
United States in 1980 of 525 million current dollars,[6]
about 25 percent higher than my "neutral" projection and
slightly below my "optimistic" projection.

Compared with these stable and projected growth trends
in China's total exports and imports of nonagricultural
goods in trade with the United States are the erratic and
unexpected Chinese imports of agricultural products (mostly
wheat, corn, oil seeds, and cotton), totaling, in million
current U.S. dollars, 0 in 1971, 62 in 1972, 648 in 1973,
656 in 1974, and 79 in 1975. China has been importing
agricultural products on a large scale since the domestic
agricultural crises in 1959-61; Chinese imports of foodstuffs (largely cereals) increasing from less than 1
percent of total imports in the 1950s to about 25 percent
of total imports in 1961-64. In general, the level of
these agricultural product imports is determined by fluctuations in domestic agricultural production. For example, the very difficult agricultural years in the early
1970s (grain output in 1972 was no higher than it had
been in 1970, and the 1970 grain output was less than 5
percent larger than it had been in 1967) obviously created
the forces which led to China's importation of over 7 million tons of grain in 1973 and again in 1974. The average level of grain imports in 1961-72 had been less than
5 million tons, an average exceeded only in the mid-1960s
following the agricultural crises in 1959-61.

The explanation of the sudden and large jump in
Chinese imports from the United States in 1973 and 1974
and their rapid decline in 1975 is the decision of the
Chinese to shift these purchases of agricultural products
(food grains, oil seeds, and cotton) to the United States
at the same time their total demand for these imports had
increased significantly and the reverse--a shift away from
the United States as a major supplier while their total
demand for these imports was declining. Two interpreta-
tions of this empirical evidence are possible: either
the Chinese view the United States as a residual source
of agricultural products in time of need or these sudden
shifts reflect changing political relations between the
United States and China. Whether for either reason, these
sudden shifts are facilitated because the commodities
involved are homogeneous commodities with several major
alternative sources of supply available to the Chinese.

This discussion of the past five years should make
clear the obstacles in trying to forecast the future for
U.S. exports to China. Foremost among these problems is

the difficult task of forecasting Chinese agricultural
production. The trend of the last decade would indicate
a rate of growth of about 2 percent and this is consistent
with the forecasts made by Alva Lewis Weisman and Dwight
Perkins in the papers published in the latest Joint
Economic Committee compendium of papers on China's economy
and with my forecast in a paper soon to be published by
the Council of Foreign Affairs.[7] Yet, China's past and
future--in the near future, at least--agricultural production reveals significant year-to-year fluctuations around
this trend, fluctuations due to unpredictable weather conditions and short-run changes in economic policies. And
it is these unpredictable fluctuations around the trend
which can be expected to determine China's demand for
agricultural product imports in any particular year.
     Even if we could predict these fluctuations, however,
there is another serious problem. Despite repeated attempts I have been unable to determine, on the basis of
the available data for the past fifteen years, a stable
relationship between these fluctuations in domestic agricultural production and imports of agricultural products,
often ending up with negative coefficients of correla-
tions. In other words, the manner in which a shortfall or
surplus in one agricultural year works its way through the
other sectors of the Chinese economy to become expressed
as a potential demand for a specific amount of agricultural products imports is too complicated to allow for a
crude functional relationship to be specified. We can,
however, state our belief with some certainty that the
inability of the Chinese to solve their agricultural
problem over the past twenty-five years and the difficulties most experts expect them to encounter in the near
future in their attempts to solve this problem will cause
China to remain a major importer of agricultural products.
Although these imports did not reveal either an upward or
downward trend over the period 1961-75, my own expectation
is that Chinese imports of agricultural products will
increase over the next decade, but not as fast as total
imports; i.e., their share in total imports will decline.
     Even if we were able to predict this potential demand
for imports of agricultural products over the near future,
however, the actual level of these imports will be subject
to the constraints of China's balance of payments and
Chinese policy on foreign borrowing. When the shortfall
in domestic supplies of agricultural products in 1974-75
led to a rapid increase in the level of imports of these
commodities, this sudden increase coincided with the
rapid increase in imports of producer goods, especially
complete plants, and China's merchandise trade account
became seriously out of balance. Knowing that their
export capacity is basically determined by their

agricultural production, that they have a policy of no
long-term foreign borrowing, and that they have practiced
a fairly conservative principle of trying to plan and control their foreign trade to achieve annual overall balance
in the merchandise trade account, I believe it was the
rapid increase in prices for their imports or, much less
likely, the failure to achieve a hoped-for rapid development of petroleum exports which led to an unplanned and
unexpected import surplus of over 1 billion current U.S.
dollars in 1974.

Whatever their prior expectations, once this deficit
had been incurred and financed by short-term credit, the
Chinese, as they have over the past twenty-five years,
reacted by making adjustments in the trade itself so as to
bring their merchandise trade into balance, not by taking
recourse to long-term borrowing abroad. In 1975, by reducing imports--mainly a reduction in agricultural product
imports--the deficit was cut in half, and the early returns
for trade in 1976 show the continuation of their efforts
to eliminate the imbalance in their total merchandise trade,
especially cutting imports of machinery and equipment from
the United States and Japan. I believe this policy of not
incurring long-term debt obligations will remain a major
principle of China's foreign trade behavior in the foreseeable future. Thus, although I expect the potential
demand for agricultural imports to increase over the next
decade, the actual level of those imports in any particular
year will be subject to the overall conditions in China's
balance of payments.

Even if we could predict accurately their actual total
agricultural imports in the near future, however, this still
would not tell us the share of those imports which will be
supplied by the United States. As is true of metals--the
Chinese switched their imports of metals from the Soviet
Union to Western European and Japanese sources of supply
in the late 1950s--agricultural products also are relatively homogenous, and the Chinese have switched their
purchases among different suppliers rather quickly. It
is in trade in commodities such as these that the Chinese
can and will--I expect--allow politics to play a considerable role. In fact, I believe politics did play a role
in their decision to make the United States the residual
supplier of agricultural products in the last three years,
increasing purchases in the United States rapidly in 1975.
I have neither the desire nor the ability to try spelling
out the various scenarios for the future of political relations between the United States and China over the next
few years, especially in light of the current scene in
Peking. However, as far as the unfortunate long-run trend
that has occurred throughout the world over the last half
century of foreign trade being incorporated among the

instruments of the Foreign Office to be used in achieving
their political objectives, China is neither the first or
worst offender.

In conclusion, Sino-American trade over the past five
years has grown within the range of my earlier, relatively
conservative, expectations, except for the unstable and
unpredictable Chinese imports of agricultural products in
1973 and 1974, and--I believe--it will still continue to
grow within those predictions; i.e., Sino-American trade
will not become a significant element of our total trade
(probably less than 0.5 percent), nor will it account for
a dominant share of China's foreign trade either (perhaps
accounting for 5-10 percent of China's exports and 10-15
percent of China's imports). Yet, this trade already has
done well what it was called upon to do--to create an
initial, visible, and meaningful link between these two
countries in the new era of detente; to facilitate the
development of normal political relations between those
countries. I wish I could report that the development of
those political relations has done as well as Sino-American trade in meeting our earlier expectations; but here
our expectations or forecasts have yet to be realized.

Notes

1. Robert F. Dernberger, "Prospects for Trade between
China and the United States," in Alexander Eckstein, ed.,
China Trade and U.S. Policy (New York: Praeger, 1971),
p. 259.

2. Ignoring the statistical problems involved, as
well as the danger of using current rather than constant
prices, the observed values for China's exports to the
United States in 1971-75 yield this time trend:

$$Y_t = -41.7 + 38.9T$$

with Y_t = the level of Chinese exports to the United States
in year t, in current million U.S. dollars, and T = the
relevant year, with T = 1 for 1971, 2 for 1972, 3 for 1973,
etc. The coefficient of correlation is 0.99+.

3. See, for example, Harry A. Cahill, The China Trade
and U.S. Tariffs (New York: Praeger, 1973).

4. CIA, China: Energy Balance Projections, A(ER)
75-75, Nov. 1975; and Kim Woodard, "The International
Energy Policies of the People's Republic of China" (Ph.d.
diss., Department of Political Science, Stanford University, Aug. 1976).

5. Again, ignoring the statistical problems involved,
as well as the danger of using current rather than constant
prices, the observed values for China's imports from the

United States in 1971-75 yield the time trend:
$$Y_t = -23.5 + 136.3T$$
with Y_t = the level of Chinese imports from the United
States in year t, in current million U.S. dollars, and T =
the relevant year, with T = 1 for 1971, 2 for 1972, 3 for
1973, etc. The coefficient of correlation is 0.57-.
   6. The observèd values for China's nonagricultural
imports from the United States in 1971-75 yield the time
trend:
$$Y_t = -86.9 + 61.1T$$
with Y_t = the level of Chinese nonagricultural imports from
the United States in year t, in current million U.S. dollars, and T = relevant year, with T = 1 for 1971, 2 for
1972, 3 for 1973, etc. The coefficient of correlation is
0.98.
   7. Alva Lewis Weisman, "China: Agriculture in the
1970's," and Dwight Perkins, "Constraints Influencing
China's Agricultural Performance," in China: A Reassessment of the Economy, Joint Economic Committee, U.S. Congress (Washington, D.C.: U.S. Government Printing Office,
1975). Robert F. Dernberger, "China's Economic Evolution
And Its Implications for the International System in the
1980's," to be published in a volume of three essays on
China and the International System by the Council on
Foreign Relations, New York.

PART III

Political and Other Aspects of China's Trade

5. China's Foreign Trade and the "Gang of Four"

Tao-tai Hsia

China's Foreign Trade in 1976

A February 10, 1977, report in the New York Times indicated
that the Japan External Trade Organization (JETRO) had
estimated China's foreign trade in 1976 at $13.1 billion
to $13.4 billion. According to JETRO, this total repre-
sented a 6 to 8 percent drop from the total value of trade
in 1975. Of the 1976 total, JETRO estimated, China's
exports constituted $7 billion to $7.2 billion, an increase
of 3 to 4 percent over the 1975 figure, and its imports
were valued at $6 billion to $6.2 billion, a decrease of
15 to 20 percent from 1975. While other sources may arrive at different estimates of the volume of China's
foreign trade in 1976, it is likely that all will record
only a slight increase in exports, a marked decline in
imports, and a small drop in overall volume of trade.

Various factors can be identified as contributing to
the waning of China's foreign trade in 1976. One of these
factors, the attitudes and activities of the "Gang of Four"
with respect to foreign trade before they were purged in
early October 1976, is one of the major topics of this
chapter. The focus on this topic is not intended to imply
that the obstacles presented by the Gang of Four were the
main factor depressing China's foreign trade in 1976. In
fact, Western observers tend to assign much more weight
to economic and financial considerations than they do to
the obstructive attitudes and activities of the Gang. It
is helpful to review some of these economic and financial
considerations before discussing the Gang's stance.

First, as a U.S. government study indicates, the
reduction of China's imports in 1976 can be regarded as a
continuation of a trend that began in 1974 in response to
an unfavorable change in China's terms of trade. It has
been emphasized that

> China's terms of trade improved substantially between
> 1970 and 1973, providing an incentive to increase
> trade, and then declined sharply in 1974 and 1975.
> The Chinese did not anticipate either the depressed
> demand for their exports, caused by the world reces-
> sion, or the sharp jump in the prices of their
> commodity imports. The crunch came in second half
> 1974. When the Chinese realized how badly their
> trade balance was deteriorating, they immediately
> took steps to cut back imports. Contracts for
> agricultural imports were canceled and deliveries
> were postponed. In 1974 and 1975 the volume of

every major commodity that China imports fell.
Whole plant purchased dropped from $1.3 billion in
1973 to $800 million in 1974 and to less than $50
million in the first nine months of 1975.[1]

Despite the cutback in imports in 1974, the People's Republic of China (PRC) accumulated in 1973 through 1975 an
uncustomary trade deficit of almost $1.5 billion.[2] The
decline in trade in 1976 hence can be regarded as in part
the result of a predictable and purposeful decision, taken
in accordance with the PRC's long-standing policy of maintaining a favorable trade balance, not to add further to
the discomforting deficit. There is another sense in which
the cutback in trade can be said to have been predictable.
Between 1972 and 1975 the Chinese made massive purchases
from the West of complete plants and their associated equipment and technology; these purchases have been calculated
to have reached almost $2.5 billion by the end of 1975.[3]
The reduction of imports in 1976 can be regarded as having
been necessary to provide the PRC a breathing spell during
which to absorb the massive purchases of the previous
years. For the PRC to have made further large purchases
in 1976, it can be argued, would have been to risk overbur-
dening the economy. It also must be recalled that 1976
was a year of natural disasters for the PRC, the most
catastophic of which was the Tangshan earthquake in July.
The full extent of the damages caused by the Tangshan
earthquake has not been disclosed to outsiders. It can
be surmised, however, that those damages had an effect on
foreign trade through their disruption of the transportation system, the mining of coal, and the production of
steel.
        Two other factors contributing to the lagging of
foreign trade in 1976 stem from the political upheavals
of the year. According to the steady stream of denunciations of the Gang of Four that has dominated Chinese media
since soon after the purge in early October 1976, one of
the chief means by which the Gang hoped to effect a capitalist restoration was through undermining the economy.
Production throughout China is said to have suffered
and, in some cases, to have come to a complete halt as a
result of the Gang's encouragement of sabotage, factional
strife, worker insubordination to management, disregard
or defiance of rational rules and regulations, inattention
to economic considerations, interference with the transportation system, etc. While neither the full extent to
which production suffered in 1976 nor the degree of the
Gang's culpability is known, it seems certain that the
Chinese economy made a comparatively poor showing in
1976,[4] and it is reasonable to assume that the state of
the domestic economy had negative effects on foreign trade.

The Gang's alleged efforts to undermine the socialist economy may be said to have had mainly indirect effects on foreign trade. In addition to these indirect effects, the apparent attempts of the Gang and their followers to influence directly the conduct of the PRC's foreign trade must be taken into account. Outsiders have long been aware that foreign trade was one of the areas of factional dispute in Peking. The recent denunciations of the Gang's attitude toward and activities in foreign trade provide materials useful to developing a deeper understanding of this conflicted area.

Both radicals and moderates have indulged in the Chinese media in polemical excesses in their respective attempts to impugn the ideological rectitude, fidelity to the thought of Mao Tse-tung, patriotism, honorable intentions, and good sense of their opponents. In the Hua administration's overall portrait of the Gang of Four, Wang Hung-wen, Chang Ch'un-ch'iao, Chiang Ch'ing, and Yao Wen-yüan have been presented as being motivated exclusively by greed for wealth and power rather than by the concern for ideological purity which was prominent in the public image they cultivated. In the area of foreign trade, the Gang's involvement has been cynically dismissed by the new administration primarily as a simple function of their overall scheme to undermine the socialist economy as a means of usurping power and restoring capitalism; secondarily, they have been portrayed as having concerned themselves with foreign trade so as to facilitate their acquiring the Western-made luxuries necessary to their decadent, bourgeois life-style.[5] The position of the Gang of Four with respect to foreign trade thus has been dismissed out of hand as being ignobly inspired and without a defensible basis in either theory or reality. Because of the polemical tone of the denunciations of the Gang, it is especially important to keep clearly in mind the broadest features of the backdrop against which the debate beween the radicals and the moderates over foreign trade took place. Most Westerners, reared as they are in technologically and economically oriented societies well integrated into an international economic order, will probably be unsympathetic to the radical position. Evaluating the radicals views on foreign trade against their immediate backdrop makes it more difficult, however, to follow the Hua administration's public lead in rejecting the radical stance outright as indefensible and irrational.

The Background to the Dispute

One need not look long for a key to understanding the central concerns in the debate between radicals and moderates over foreign trade. It first is to be pointed out that the U.S. dollar value of the PRC's foreign trade increased from \$4,720 million in 1971 to \$14,320 million in 1975.[6] The Hua administration has characterized this abrupt and dramatic increase in foreign trade as follows: "In 1975 our country's total exports and imports were 13 times those of 1950, the initial period of the People's Republic, and more than 3 times those of 1965, the year before the Great Proletarian Cultural Revolution."[7] In such a formulation the attempt of the Hua administration to gloss over the abruptness of the increase in foreign trade in the 1970s and to imply that the increase came as a result of, rather than in spite of, the Cultural Revolution, is transparent. Knowing that the radical faction has been most strongly identified with the policy of self-reliance, the outsider need only to examine the gross foreign trade figures for the 1970s to realize that one of the major issues in the debate over foreign trade has been the volume of the PRC's trade, that is, the extent to which the PRC should involve its economy with those of other countries. Second, it is to be pointed out that in 1975, 57 percent of the PRC's foreign trade was with the developed countries, largely Japan and the Western nations.[8] In light of the history of the PRC's enmity toward Japan and the West, one easily can surmise that the direction of China's foreign trade has been an issue. Third, prior to 1972 the PRC was not an exporter of crude oil. Between 1973 and 1975, "China delivered in increasing amounts a total of 80 million barrels of crude oil to Japan."[9] In this short period petroleum sales came to "constitute China's largest single source of foreign exchange."[10] Further, as stated above, between 1972 and 1975 the PRC purchased complete plants valued at almost U.S. \$2.5 billion.[11] In view of these figures, one readily can imagine that the composition of China's exports and imports was a third issue over which the radicals and moderates were at odds.

Self-Reliance or Isolation?

The dramatic and swift changes evident in gross figures on China's foreign trade in the early 1970s suggest that the clashes between the radicals and moderates would have involved the volume, direction, and composition of the PRC's foreign trade. The Hua administration's public indictments of the radical stance suggest the same conclusion. At times, however, these public indictments tend to portray the issue as having been whether China should engage in foreign trade at all. The radicals' position is represented as having been essentially an

isolationist one. One wonders whether the representation
of the radicals as isolationists results from their opponents' need to exaggerate the radical attitude for polemical effect, or whether the radicals in fact were forced
into an essentially isolationist position by their need,
as a minority without a strong power base, to attack every
initiative of the moderates. In their own published representation of their position, the radicals rejected the isolationist label. In their attacks on Teng Hsiao-p'ing, the
radicals stated the crux of their position (and overstated
Teng's position) as follows:

> We hold that, under the guidance of the principle
> of independence and self-reliance, it is necessary
> to import some foreign techniques and equipment on
> the basis of equality and mutual benefit and in
> accordance with the needs of our country's socialist
> revolution and construction. But we absolutely
> cannot place our hopes for realizing the four moderni-
> zations on imports. If we do not rely mainly on our
> own efforts, but, as Teng Hsiao-p'ing advocated, rely
> solely on importing foreign techniques, copying
> foreign designs and technological processes and
> patterning our equipment on foreign models, we will
> for ever trail behind foreigners and our country's
> development of technology and even its entire
> national economy will fall under the control of
> foreign monopoly capital.[12]

The New Leadership's Characterization of the Gang's Position

The radical attack on the PRC's foreign trade policies has
been presented after the purge as having been comprehensive.
An article in the April 3, 1977, Hung ch'i (Red Flag)
charges: "Practicing metaphysics frantically, the 'gang of
four' described normal imports as 'slavish' and rational
exports as 'national betrayal.' With an ulterior motive
they set independence, keeping the initiative in our hands
and self-reliance against foreign trade."[13] They are said
to have argued that the Ministry of Foreign Trade "unrestrainedly imported what China can produce and limitlessly
exported what is badly needed at home."[14] The Gang's
overall evaluation of the composition of the PRC's foreign
trade was that the Ministry of Foreign Trade had "tried
to turn China into the imperialist countries' dumping
ground, raw material base, repair workshop and outlet
for investments."[15]
   While the gang is thus represented as having made
comprehensive attacks on foreign trade policies, their
displeasure seems to have focused on two issues: the import

of complete plants and Western technology and the export
of oil.

With respect to complete plants and technology, the
Gang has been charged generally with having

> willfully distorted the policy of independence,
> keeping the initiative in our hands and achieving
> rejuvenation through self-reliance, and indiscrim-
> inately rejected all foreign technology and equip-
> ment. They always attached the label "worshipping
> things foreign and fawning on foreigners" and "the
> doctrine of trailing behind at a snail's pace" to
> some needed import items. They described needed
> technological exchanges conducted with various
> countries of the world under the principle of
> equality and mutual benefit as "prostrating at
> the feet of the Western bourgeoisie and being
> willing to crawl behind others every step of the
> way.[16]

Probably more to the point, Chang Ch'un-ch'iao is reported
to have "blustered" at a conference: "We are importing too
many major items, a whole bunch of things all at once."[17]

Particularly bitter were the Gang's attacks against
the export of the PRC's oil to Japan as "selling out the
natural resources of the state." Chiang Ch'ing is said to
have "declared that 'by exporting petroleum China is
shifting the international energy crisis on to the Chinese
people,' and it 'has saved the first and second worlds.'"[18]
With regard to oil, the Gang is charged with not having
limited itself to verbal attacks. An extensive passage in
a January 13, 1977, release of the New China News Agency
reads:

> Originally, our country's comprehensive 1976 plan
> for a balance in fuel and raw materials...had already
> been approved by the central authorities. However,
> the "gang of four" stirred up trouble behind the
> scenes while outwardly approving it. They sent
> orders to their minions in Shanghai and Liaoning
> to make successive "urgent requests" to the central
> departments concerned, apply pressure on others
> with such labels as "disrupting production and
> sabotaging revolution" and "smearing the movement
> to repulse the right deviationist wind to reverse
> verdicts," and willfully change the coal-consuming
> enterprises into oil-consuming ones with the
> ulterior motive of deliberately creating a situa-
> tion in which there was an urgent need for oil.
> Having thus disrupted the state's unified plan,
> they then made unfounded counter-charges to
> frame foreign trade personnel.

In 1976 alone, that sworn follower of the "gang
of four" in Liaoning had willfully increased the
number of oil-consuming units by more than a hundred.
Shanghai's crude oil consumption for 1976 exceeded
the plan by 1 million tons. The "gang of four"
even disregarded the state's unified allocation plan
and flagrantly "made false reports on the situation
on the battlefield." Under the pretext of "protect-
ing Shanghai," it forced the central departments
concerned to give its approval to intercept crude
oil at Shanghai harbor destined for the fraternal
provinces and municipalities. In 1976 it intercepted
13 tankers at Wusungkou bound for Maoming in Kwangtung, Nanking in Kiangsu, Changling in Hunan and
other localities and seized a total of 200,000 tons
of crude oil.[19]

As a result of the Gang's interference, "some enterprises in
other provinces and municipalities were compelled to halt
work and stop production," "some oil refineries 'had no
rice for the cooker,'" and "in some localities the irrigation and drainage machines stopped running right at the
crucial flood prevention time." Even oil exports were
said to have been affected, an event which harmed China's
"international credibility and had negative effects both
politically and economically."[20]
    As in other areas of party and state activity, the
Gang apparently attempted to gain a foothold in the foreign
trade apparatus. In an article in the first 1977 issue of
China's Foreign Trade, the Mass Criticism Group of the China
Council for the Promotion of International Trade charged:
"They used the power and position they had usurped in the
Party Central Committee to stretch their tentacles into
some foreign trade departments. In the isolated foreign
trade organizations under their control, they formed a
factional group, did as they liked and behaved quite
arbitrarily. They openly refused to carry out directives
from the Party Central Committee; they forced their views
on higher levels and fraternal organizations."[21] Having
made some inroads in the foreign trade organizations, the
Gang "clamoured about taking organizational 'measures' to
'change the leading bodies' and made preparations organi-
zationally to seize power. Seizing power in foreign trade
departments was part of their scheme for an all-round
seizure of power."[22]
    A passage in the January 13, 1977, NCNA release quoted
above leads one to wonder to what extent officials in the
PRC who are not intimately involved with foreign trade
are knowledgeable of the PRC's activities in foreign trade.
One of the gang's purposes in penetrating the foreign trade
apparatus seems to have been gaining access to information

about foreign trade which then could be used in a "lobbying"
effort for its cause. In the NCNA account, the Gang is
said to have

> adopted the wicked tactics of placing their people
> in the Ministry of Foreign Trade, foreign trade
> departments in a number of localities, and the Can-
> ton trade fair to steal state secrets and economic
> information like spies. These people wrote and
> gathered sinister materials and then sent them to
> Yao Wen-yuan for his personal copying. To openly
> incite trouble, this literary scoundrel personally
> wrote such sinister words on the materials as "if
> great attention is still unpaid to this, the workers
> may take their own measures because they extremely
> hate the practice of squandering the fruits of their
> blood and sweat to curry favor with foreign capi-
> talists." Using the power usurped by him, Wang
> Hung-wen immediately distributed these carefully
> produced sinister materials to the representatives
> of various provinces and municipalities and various
> departments and ministries under the central
> authorities attending a conference in order to
> confuse the people everywhere.[23]

Once the Gang was purged, staff members and workers in
foreign trade are said to have been "relieved of their mental burden." If all the charges of the Hua administration
against the Gang are to be believed, one can well imagine
that China's foreign trade cadres had been working in a
strained, "no-win" atmosphere. A telling account in
Hung ch'i, April 3, 1977, indicated:

> With a view to undermining our country's exports,
> the "gang of four" also made a host of accusations·
> and created confusion with respect to pricing,[24]
> trade practices, managerial procedures and many
> other problems. When you improved the quality,
> variety, design and packaging of export commodities
> in order to suit the customs and habits and level of
> consumption of other countries and nations and to
> meet the needs of the international market, they
> attacked you for "waiting on the foreign bourgeoisie."
> When you made use of some conventional practices
> applied in international trade, they charged you with
> "right capitulation." When you exported arts and
> crafts, they said you promoted "four olds." When
> you exported some farm and subsidiary produce,
> they said you "ignore domestic demand." When you
> exported raw materials, they said you "sell out
> natural resources." When you exported finished
> goods, they said you "sell out labor." In short,

everything you did was wrong. Thus they sabotaged
our country's socialist foreign trade with any
means that justified the end.[25]

The Hua Administration's Policy toward Foreign Trade

Each of the recent exposés of the Gang of Four's interference with China's foreign trade has included a statement of
the Hua administration's basic policies toward foreign trade.
These statements feature the assertion that "China's foreign trade all along was conducted under Chairman Mao's
solicitous concern and Premier Chou's direct leadership."[26]
Having thus established the legitimacy of past policies
and practices, the statements then indicate that they
basically will be continued under the new leadership.
The following is a typical statement of what are to be the
general principles of China's foreign trade under Hua:
"Our basis of building socialism is self-reliance. We must
uphold the policy of independence, keeping the initiative
in our hands and achieving rejuvenation through self-reliance, rely on the strength and wisdom of the Chinese
people themselves, rely on our country's internal accumu-
lations and utilize our country's natural resources in
carrying out socialist construction and developing science
and technology."[27] The statement hastens to add, however,
that self-reliance does not mean shunning imports and not
learning from other countries. It is emphatic in its
denial of the notion that importing technology and equipment from other countries means "worshipping things foreign and fawning on foreigners." To give authority to
the import of advanced technology and equipment from other
countries, the statement quotes approvingly Mao's assertion in "On the Ten Major Relationships" that "our policy
is to learn from the strong points of all nations and all
countries, learn all that is genuinely good in the political, economic, scientific and technological fields and
in literature and art. But we must learn with an analytical and critical eye, not blindly, and we mustn't copy
everything indiscriminately and transplant mechanically."[28]
The rationale for importing advanced technology and equipment is saving time. While "the Chinese people can certainly make scientific and technological inventions and crea-
tions as well as foreigners and may even surpass them in
some respects," "there is a problem of racing against
time, for speed."[29]
The necessity of continuing exports is strongly
affirmed. Basic guidelines for exports are set forth:

When it comes to the arrangement of internal and
external marketing, important materials relevant

> to national planning and the people's livelihood
> must be exported in limited quantities; where goods
> are in internal and external demand and are in rela-
> tively tight supply, active efforts must be made to
> develop production so that a portion may be squeezed
> out for export; commodities which are not in great
> demand in the domestic market may basically be
> allocated for export. Efforts must be made to
> "squeeze out," and if this is properly done, there
> will not be considerable adverse effect on the
> domestic market and more may be squeezed out for
> export.[30]

The conflict between production for the domestic market
and production for export will be alleviated, the new
administration contends, by increasing production. With a
greater abundance of products, there will be less sense of
loss when goods are exported.

The new administration hopes also gradually to change
the composition of China's exports. "We need to constantly
increase," it contends,

> the proportion of our exports in industrial and
> mining products to gradually change the long-
> standing situation in which our exports are mainly
> agricultural products, handicrafts and local
> specialty products. At present, the proportion
> of industrial and mining products in our exports
> has expanded from 30 percent in the early post-
> liberation days to 65 percent. This shows that
> the working class of our country has made tremen-
> dous achievements in building the socialist indus-
> try by carrying forward the spirit of self-reli-
> ance and working energetically for the prosperity
> of our country.[31]

Dismissing as ridiculous the notion that China's export of small quantities of oil could have saved the
Western countries from the energy crisis, the new administration indicates that the export of oil will be continued,
but it is silent with respect to the quantities to be
exported. "The export of oil," it asserts, "is not only
for obtaining foreign exchange, but, what is more important, to implement Chairman Mao's revolutionary line on
foreign affairs."[32] Another source indicates more
specifically that "our oil exports play a certain role in
opposing the two hegemonic powers of the Soviet Union and
the United States, in supporting the struggle of the Third
World people and in trading for construction materials to
help promote our country's construction."[33] It is telling
that no more specific statement is made about the manner
in which the export of oil carries out Chairman Mao's

revolutionary line in foreign affairs. Indeed, if one read
only the recent Chinese statements on foreign trade, one
would never know that Japan is the major purchaser of
Chinese oil.

There are interesting omissions in the Hua administration's recent statements on foreign trade policy. In the
1975 document "Several Questions on the Speeding Up of
Industrial Development," Teng Hsiao-p'ing not only gave
an expression of strong support for the continued development of foreign trade, but he also took two positions
highly unacceptable to the radicals. Teng is quoted by
his radical opponents as having stated: "In order to speed
up the development of our extraction of coal and petroleum,
under the condition of equality and mutual benefit, in
accordance with such usual practices of international
trade as deferred payment and payment by installations,
[we should] sign long-term contracts with foreign countries, establish certain productive points for which they
will supply the necessary appropriate, modern complete
plants, and pay them back later with our coal and crude
oil."[34] Two features of Teng's position aroused the
radicals' ire. First was the signing of long-term (usually
understood to mean more than five years) contracts, a practice which the PRC had theretofore avoided. Second of the
objectionable features was increased reliance on oil
exports in foreign trade and the creation of a direct
linkage between the import of complete plants and the
export of oil in payment. In the primary sources gathered
for this discussion, the Hua administration was silent about
the matter of long-term contracts. While it affirmed both
that the import of advanced technology and complete plants
would be continued and that China would continue to export
oil and hopefully coal, it almost always avoided linking
discussion of these two matters. The generally careful
separation of discussion of the import of plants and
technology and the export of fuels would seem to indicate
that such "product payback" schemes are still a touchy
matter. David L. Denny of the Bureau of East-West Trade,
Department of Commerce, has written:

> The most interesting aspect of the campaign against
> Teng was the charge that he apparently considered
> long-term contracts with Western firms for techno-
> logy, plant, and equipment for natural resource
> development. Part or all of repayment was to be
> in the form of raw material exports (produce pay-
> back). It is not known how seriously the Chinese
> considered such proposals nor is it known whether
> recent political changes again make it possible
> to discuss such arrangements. Other attacks on
> foreign trade policy were publically refuted in

late 1976, but the possibility of using "product
payback" to finance complete plant imports has not
reemerged.[35]

The Hua administration has explicitly rejected some
types of developmental schemes. "China," the new administration has asserted, "is an independent socialist country.
It has never allowed, and will never allow, the import of
foreign capital or joint development with capitalist countries of the natural resources in our country or in other
countries. It has never permitted, and will never permit,
enterprises operated jointly with foreign capitalists,
leasing territorial land and sea sovereignty to other
countries."[36] Again, "we are resolutely opposed to the
exploitation of our national resources by foreign capital.
We have never operated any joint enterprises with foreign
countries, and do not accept loans from other countries.
China has neither internal nor external debts."[37]

Trade since the Purge of the Gang

As a result of the purge of the Gang of Four, China's
Foreign Trade observed in early 1977, "the excellent situation has opened up bright prospects for foreign trade."[38]
Foreign observers speculated about how bright the prospects
actually were.

By mid-1977 news of a few major transactions had
appeared in the Western press. At the end of October 1976
it was reported that the United States had agreed to issue
a license for the sale of two Control Data Corporation Cyber
172 computers and associated equipment to the PRC. The
United States conceded both that the computers had possible
defense uses and that the provisions for monitoring and
inspecting the computers were less stringent than those
previously required for Communist countries.[39] China and
Japan were reported to have concluded in April a long-
term agreement on the exchange of Chinese crude oil for
Japanese technology, machinery, and high-quality steel.
No details of the agreement were available, so it cannot
be established whether the agreement was a product-payback
scheme such as was proposed by Teng.[40] In May it was
announced that China planned to send a delegation to the
United States to examine American petroleum equipment.[41]
In July, China was reported to have resumed the purchase
of drilling equipment from the United States.[42] By early
July, China had contracted for the purchase of almost
7 million metric tons of wheat from Canada, Australia,
and Argentina, and its leaders reportedly had indicated
their intention to resume purchases of U.S. wheat.[43]

Li Chiang, the PRC's minister of foreign trade, was

reported to have indicated to an American trade delegation
that trade would show big increases in 1978.[44] Some
observers were of the opinion that lack of normalization
of Sino-American relations constituted a major obstacle
to the fuller development of trade between the PRC and the
United States. In May it was revealed that U.S. and
Chinese officials had resumed secret talks on the resolution
of the claims/assets issue.[45] If an agreement were reached
on the claims/assets problem, there still would remain the
obstacle posed by the PRC's not enjoying most-favored-nation
status with respect to U.S. tariffs. It is unlikely that
the PRC's emigration policy would satisfy the criteria
set forth by the Jackson-Vanik Amendment to the Trade Reform
Act of 1974 for the granting of most-favored-nation
status.[46]

Conclusion

In evaluating the prospects for foreign trade under the Hua
administration, one must consider, of course, matters
beyond its direct policy on foreign trade. The Hua administration's vigorous commitment to the realization of the
four modernizations, its support for scientific and technological research and development, its more conventional
approach to education, and its promotion of "rational rules
and regulations" in industry also must be taken into
account, for all ultimately will have effects on foreign
trade. One also must consider the fact that many demands
are being placed on China's resources: modernization of
the armed forces, mechanization of agriculture, improvement of the living standard of the citizenry, etc. It is
especially important to take into account the likelihood
that even the purge of the radicals will not result in
China's departing significantly from its past conservative
policies with respect to the financing of foreign trade.
Taken together, all these factors seem to point to a
genuine commitment to the development of foreign trade
under the new administration, but only modest increases
in its levels for the foreseeable future.

Notes

1. U.S. Central Intelligence Agency, People's
Republic of China: International Trade Handbook,
Oct. 1976, p. 6.
    2. Ibid., p. 13.
    3. David L. Denny and Frederic M. Surls, "China's
Foreign Financial Liabilities," China Business Review
4, no. 2 (March-April 1977): p. 17 and table 3.

    4. Fox Butterfield, "China Said to Falter in Its
Economy in '76," New York Times, March 20, 1977, and
Peter Griffiths, "China Bluntly Details Major Problems of
Food, Energy, Industrial Output," Washington Post, March
12, 1977.
    5. See "NCNA on 'Gang' Sabotage of Foreign Trade,"
Foreign Broadcast Information Service, Daily Report:
People's Republic of China, Jan. 14, 1977, p. E8, for
specifics on the Gang's use of its influence in foreign
trade to import luxuries.
    6. People's Republic of China: International Trade
Handbook, p. 13.
    7. "NCNA on 'Gang' Sabotage of Foreign Trade," p.
E2.
    8. People's Republic of China: International Trade
Handbook, p. 14.
    9. Chu-yuan Cheng, "China's Future as an Oil Exporter,"
New York Times, April 4, 1976.
    10. "'76 Oil Output Up 13%, China Says," New York Times,
Jan. 7, 1977.
    11. Denny and Surls, p. 17.
    12. Kao Lu and Chang Ko, "Comments on Teng Hsiao-
p'ing's Economic Ideas of the Comprador Bourgeoisie,"
Peking Review, no. 35 (Aug. 27, 1976): 8-9.
    13. Kuo Mao-yen, "Exposé of the Plot of the 'Gang of
Four' in Attacking Foreign Trade," Hung ch'i [Red Flag],
no. 4 (April 3, 1977), English translation in Selections
from People's Republic of China Magazines, nos. 922-23
(April 29-May 6, 1977): 69.
    14. Kuo Chi, "Foreign Trade: Why the 'Gang of Four'
Created Confusion," Peking Review, no. 9 (Feb. 25, 1977):
17.
    15. Ibid.
    16. Kuo Mao-yen, p. 70.
    17. Kuo Chi, p. 17.
    18. Ibid.
    19. "NCNA on 'Gang' Sabotage of Foreign Trade," p. E5.
    20. Ibid.
    21. "Settle Accounts with the Criminal 'Gang of Four'
and Develop Socialist Foreign Trade," China's Foreign Trade,
no. 1 (1977): 2.
    22. Kuo Chi, p. 18.
    23. "NCNA on 'Gang Sabotage of Foreign Trade," p. E4.
    24. This passage does not take up the matter of pricing
after having introduced it here. Another source indicates,
however, that "they wantonly slandered our export prices
as being too low and so giving money away to capitalists"
and slapped on "capitulationist" and "national betrayal"
labels ("Settle Accounts with the Criminal 'Gang of Four'
and Develop Socialist Foreign Trade," p. 3).

25. Kuo Mao-yen, p. 73.
26. Kuo Chi, p. 16.
27. Kuo Mao-yen, p. 69.
28. Mao Tse-tung, "On the Ten Major Relationships,"
Peking Review, no. 1 (Jan. 1, 1977): 23.
29. Kuo Mao-yen, p. 70.
30. Ibid., pp. 71-72.
31. "NCNA on 'Gang'Sabotage of Foreign Trade," p. E7.
32. Kuo Mao-yen, p. 72.
33. "NCNA on 'Gang' Sabotage of Foreign Trade," p. E6.
34. "Selected Comments on 'Several Questions on the
Speeding Up of Industrial Development,'" Hsueh hsi yü p'i
p'an [Study and Criticism], no. 4 (April 1976): 30.
35. Denny and Surls, p. 20.
36. Kuo Mao-yen, p. 72.
37. "Settle Accounts with the Criminal 'Gang of Four'
and Develop Socialist Foreign Trade," p. 4.
38. Ibid., p. 2.
39. Leslie H. Gelb, "U.S. Agrees to Sell China a
Computer with Defense Uses," New York Times, Oct. 29, 1976.
40. Reuter's dispatch from Peking in Lien ho jih pao
[United Journal], June 29, 1977.
41. Lee Lescaze, "China May Inspect U.S. Oil Rigs,"
Washington Post, May 28, 1977.
42. Jay Mathews, "China Resumes U.S. Drilling Equipment Purchases," Washington Post, July 5, 1977.
43. Jay Mathews, "China Seen Eying U.S. Grain Purchases," Washington Post, July 9, 1977.
44. Fox Butterfield, "The China Trade: Hopes for
Growth," New York Times, Jan. 30, 1977.
45. "U.S., Chinese Talk of Settling Claims to
Facilitate Trade," Washington Post, May 3, 1977.
46. On the claims/assets problem and most-favored-
nation status, see Stanley B. Lubman, "Trade between the
U.S. and the People's Republic of China: Practice, Policy,
and Law," Law and Policy in International Business 8, no.
1 (1976): 55-58, 53-55.

6. China's Oil Policy
Jerome Alan Cohen and Choon-ho Park

In mid-1975, when China appeared to be following the path
toward rapid modernization prescribed by Premier Chou
En-lai in his speech to the Fourth National People's Congress in January of that year,[1] we completed an introductory study of the country's rise to prominence as a potential oil power.[2] At this writing, just two years later,
the party line continues to preach Chou's call for modernization and, as a concomitant, to emphasize the increasingly
important role of oil in China's development.[3] In Peking,
a recent play dramatizing the struggle to open up China's
biggest oilfield, Taching, in the early 1960s has been
widely acclaimed,[4] and Chinese films, essays, and novels
are exploring the same theme.[5] Official news dispatches
claim the discovery of new oil- and gas-bearing structures,[6]
and there have been reports of offshore drilling in the
South China Sea in addition to the Gulf of Pohai and the
shallows of the Yellow Sea.[7] The People's Republic has
offered Japanese business leaders a long-term trade agreement for the sale of Chinese crude and other natural resources,[8] and it has sent a delegation of experts in oil
and gas extraction to the United States to scrutinize
American-made petroleum equipment.[9] Signs abound that
China is bent upon significantly expanding oil production
as a major means of vindicating new Party Chairman Hua
Kuo-feng's boast that "the proletariat of the East can
accomplish whatever the bourgeoisie of the West can accomplish, and with better results."[10]
     Thus China's oil policy appears to have changed little
between 1975 and 1977. Yet, as every student of Chinese
affairs knows, there was anything but continuity during
this brief period. Indeed, in a remarkably short span, the
wheel can be said to have come full circle.
     The death of Chou En-lai in January 1976 initiated a
chain of events that jeopardized the fulfillment of his
plan "to accomplish the comprehensive modernization of
agriculture, industry, national defense and science and
technology before the end of the century."[11] The ouster
of Chou's heir apparent, Vice-Premier Teng Hsiao-ping
in April 1976 indicated that what foreigners call the
"radical" faction had gained the upper hand in the struggle over policy and power and that its less conventional
economic development strategy -- one that advocated only
modest foreign cooperation and downgraded the importance
of oil -- would prevail. These political upheavals were
soon accompanied by the most devastating earthquakes to
hit China in over four hundred years, which caused not
only profound suffering and loss of life but also grave

economic and political dislocations that adversely affected
the production of oil as well as other resources.

The death of Mao Tse-tung in September, although
apparently the ultimate in the series of calamities that
befell the PRC in 1976, actually precipitated another
180-degree turn of the wheel. It made possible October's
stunning coup against the radical leadership, the "Gang of
Four," and set in motion both the gradual reemergence of
Teng Hsiao-p'ing and the strong reaffirmation of the economic policies with which he and his mentor, Chou En-lai, are
associated. This new or, to be more precise, renewed
trend has again pushed oil to center stage, leading the
minister of petroleum and chemical industries, Kang
Shih-en, to tell 7,000 delegates to the extraordinary
National Conference on Learning from Taching in Industry,
held in April-May 1977, that China will outstrip the United
States and advance to the front ranks of the world's oil
industry.[12] Indeed, for symbolic purposes the conference--
the culmination of a series recently held to launch the
postponed Fifth Five-Year Plan--originally met at Taching
in northeastern China, the site of the country's largest
oil field, which is again being propagandized as the model
for all of the nation's industrial units.

How does out mid-1975 appraisal of China's emerging
oil potential square with the events and revelations of the
past two years? Faithful to the Chinese belief in progress
through criticism and self-criticism, we will briefly survey the situation, reviewing the analytical categories
employed in our 1975 introductory essay--reserves, production, domestic demand, exports and foreign trade, and
implications for China's foreign policy.

                              Reserves

We really know little more now than we did two years ago
about China's oil reserves. China has not issued official
data on reserves since the Cultural Revolution of 1966-69.
Although in 1973 Peking announced that Chinese reserves
were "third in the world," it is far from clear what this
claim purported to mean, not to mention what it was based
upon.[13] In the spring of 1977 PRC leaders issued a series
of even vaguer optimistic statements, again without sub-
stantiating detail. Minister Kang Shih-en, echoing a
prophecy made by Chairman Mao two decades ago, predicted
that in the not-too-distant future China's oil industry
will exceed America's and that, given China's rich endow-
ment of oil and other natural resources, its future is much
brighter than that of the United States. Kang stated that
the PRC has "abundant oil reserves which provide it with
plenty of room to develop to the full."[14] Vice-Premier

Yu Ch'iu-li, chairman of the State Planning Commission and
formerly petroleum minister, told the national industrial
conference that the PRC "should build some ten more oilfields as big as Taching within this century."[15] Chinese
sources claim that the vice-premier's statement was not an
empty one and that the authorities have already begun to
implement plans to establish ten new petroleum centers.[16]
Since in 1976 Taching produced perhaps 38 million metric
tons (mmt), or roughly 45 percent of China's total output
that year,[17] the assumption seems to be that there are ample
reserves to draw upon elsewhere. Minister Kang proudly
proclaimed that "through self-reliance we have exploded the
[Western experts'] myth that significant petroleum reserves
are not to be found in continental sedimentary rocks," and
he said that China would carry out further large-scale oil
prospecting both onshore and offshore.[18]
    Of course, even countries that enjoy access to highly
advanced technology find it difficult to arrive at a rea-
sonably precise estimate of oil deposits. Allowances for
"tolerable error" have sometimes turned out to be intoler-
ably high. For example, one estimate of oil and gas reserves in the Atlantic continental shelf of the United
States was found to be five times higher than later surveys
thought appropriate.[19] China, which still lacks advanced
oil technology, especially for offshore oil, must find it
immensely difficult to formulate useful reserve figures,
and perhaps this is why the PRC, never a government to
publish voluminous economic figures, for over a decade
has been even less specific about its oil reserves than
about other aspects of its oil industry.
    In view of the PRC's policy of maintaining a closed
society, it is impossible for foreigners to make an accurate estimate of what Peking itself is still trying to
determine. Even exploration by foreign operators in the
offshore waters beyond China's territorial sea has been
inhibited because of disputes over continental shelf
boundaries.[20] Moreover, the always troublesome problem
of defining terms such as "confirmed," "recoverable," and
"possible" deposits becomes more so in the context of
China, which not only has its own system for classifying
reserves but also does not share the premises of open,
bourgeois societies. For example, whether onshore or
offshore, a private company's recovery of oil has to be
not only technologically feasible but also economically
profitable. A planned economy like China's, where production decisions need not be dictated to the same degree by
a concern for profit, may regard certain deposits as
"recoverable" even though they would not be so regarded in
capitalist nations. Similarly, other factors, such as
freedom from environmental pressure groups, enable China
to rely on its own methods and standards in deciding

whether the extraction of oil is feasible.

While recognizing that "there probably is greater
uncertainty in estimating oil reserves in China than for
any other region of the world" and that "no estimate or
set of estimates has won widespread acceptance," a June
1977 appraisal by the U.S. Central Intelligence Agency,
after reviewing the efforts of other outside observers,
concludes:

> The size of China's total oil reserves--onshore
> liquid, offshore liquid, and on onshore shale--is
> still unknown. Analysis of the limited body of
> information available on onshore liquid reserves,
> performed both on a statistical probability basis
> and by totaling estimates done field by field and
> structure by structure, has yielded broad agreement
> on a range centering on about 40 BB [billion bar-
> rels] of ultimately recoverable reserves, with the
> possibility that there may be as much as 100 BB.
> In comparison, as of mid-1976, remaining proved
> plus probable reserves were estimated to be 390 BB
> in the Middle East, 64 BB in Africa, 47 BB in North
> America, and 42 BB in Latin America.
> China's onland reserves, though considerable,
> cannot support predictions of China becoming a world
> oil power....
> Offshore reserves, although possibly very large,
> are as yet the subject of conjecture only. Even
> if very large, they may prove difficult and expen-
> sive to locate and extract. Neither the Chinese nor
> foreigners have yet acquired enough data on off-
> shore sedimentary deposits to make valid estimates.
> Predictions about China's future as an oil power
> based on exploitation of offshore deposits are
> premature.
> China's large shale deposits will be irrelevant
> in the next 10-20 years. The exploitation of shale
> would be prohibitively expensive and irrational as
> long as liquid oil is available.[21]

This conclusion, although cautious, does not fully
convey the CIA's pessimism concerning Chinese reserves.
That becomes apparent only when the study considers the PRC's
expanding level of crude output, which it predicts will
exhaust the country's prime reserves in the north and northeastern regions, from which about 80 percent of output has
come, within ten to fifteen years, depending upon whether
the annual rate of increase continues to be the 20 percent
sustained until 1976 or as little as 10 percent.[22] If
this prediction proves accurate, the PRC will plainly
need the "ten more oilfields as big as Taching within
this century" that it is planning. Thus China is under

great pressure to continue discovering promising, even if
increasingly remote, onshore reserves and to intensify the
search for seabed oil, barely in its preliminary stage, in
the hope of confirming the enormous additional reserves
that many believe to lie offshore. Otherwise the optimism
of the current leaders will not be vindicated.

    But what can be said about crude oil production
prospects?

Production

Our 1975 essay, after emphasizing the inadequacy of Chinese
statistics and a variety of other factors that made prediction especially hazardous, estimated that the PRC's crude
oil production in 1980 would probably be "somewhat in excess of 200 million tons." That forecast was based on
two assumptions. One was that 1974 production was approximately 70 mmt, a figure that we recognized might actually
have been considerably higher or lower than the actual.
The second assumption was "that, barring another political
upheaval of the magnitude of the Cultural Revolution--an
eventuality that cannot be dismissed, oil production will
continue to increase at an average annual rate of roughly
20 percent."[23]

    Although some observers predicted that China would
produce as much as 400 mmt by 1980,[24] an estimate we termed
far too optimistic, a number of others believed that a
200 mmt estimate was itself too optimistic.[25] The apprai-
sals of 1974 production by the latter group were less sanguine than ours, and they also doubted whether the PRC would
be able to maintain an average annual increase of 20 percent
as the production base expands.

    By the time the conference that gave rise to this study
was held in September 1976, the pessimists were riding high.
Although 1975 oil production had continued to increase at
the 20 percent rate,[26] the growth rate for the first half
of 1976 had fallen sharply. In part this was attributable
to political unrest created by "the struggles between the two
lines," which affected industrial production, rail transport, and other aspects of the economy more than outsiders
realized. Even more upsetting than the turmoil itself was
the fact that the radicals appeared to have captured the
dominant position and were using their influence to oppose
the high priority that oil production had long been
assigned in national investment policy. Moreover, the
radicals were insisting on a narrow interpretation of the
PRC's policy of "self-reliance," one that sought to limit
imports of foreign equipment required to enhance oil production rapidly and to restrict exports of oil required
to pay for the imports.[27] As they put it: "To use our

country's mineral reserves and labor with technology and
equipment provided by foreign capitalists and let foreign
bosses reap a huge fortune--such things had been done
before, by Li Hung-chang, Yuan Shih-kai, and the enemy
of the people Chiang Kai-shek. We will never forget those
days when foreign bosses were fattened by the blood and
sweat of Chinese workers. If economic independence is
lost, it will also be impossible to maintain political
independence."[28] In an attempt to make it seem that their
version of self-reliance had been responsible for China's
economic success, the radicals argued that there was no need
to risk becoming "an economic appendage of imperialism"
because "our petroleum industry has grown at the average
annual rate of over 20 percent over the last 15 years,
thanks to self-reliance, and its fast speed even our
enemies cannot deny."[29]
        The radicals' effort to channel capital investment
away from petroleum production received nonideological
support when in mid-1976 the Tangshan earthquake devastated
China's largest coal-mining complex and required substantial
additional state investment to restore the coal industry.[30]
This extraordinary natural disaster, a factor unanticipated
by all commentators, only inflicted modest direct damage
upon the nearby Takang oilfield, but damage to railroads,
pipelines, factories, and other facilities undoubtedly had
an indirect impact upon oil production.
        The October 1976 coup against the radical leaders now
known as the Gang of Four did not immediately bring about
an observable increase in oil production. Indeed, the
nationwide political campaign against them and their
supporters further disrupted an economy that was already in
serious difficulty not only because of political unrest
and natural disasters but also because of worker apathy,
management inefficiency, and lack of equipment. Oil production also undoubtedly reflected reduced foreign demand for
China's oil, to which we shall subsequently refer. Amid
all these circumstances it is impressive that China managed
to increase petroleum production by as much as 13 percent
during its most calamitous year, especially when the rate
of increase of overall GNP fell at least by almost half to
slightly over 3 percent and industrial production probably
grew at most by only 4 percent rather than the annual
average of 10 percent.[31] The depressing 1976 picture
dissipated whatever chance China may have had of vindicating our earlier estimate that 1980 oil production might be
somewhat over 200 mmt. Yet how far off the mark that estimate will be remains unclear. The Hua Kuo-feng government's
vigorous repudiation of the economic development policies
of the Gang of Four, including their alleged attempts to
slander and sabotage the nation's development of oil,[32]

suggests that once again high priority has been assigned to
capital investment in oil production facilities and that
considerable emphasis will again be given to importing
foreign equipment and technology to speed the pace of oil
production. Within weeks after the fall of Mao's widow
and her cohorts, Minister of Foreign Trade Li Chiang and
his deputies were telling visitors that China would soon
resume large-scale purchases of foreign equipment and that,
even though the Fifth Five-Year Plan had been delayed, they
still hoped to achieve all of its objectives by the end
of the original period in 1980.[33] Businessmen attending the
spring 1977 Canton trade fair and delegates to the national
industrial conference were also told that the PRC cannot
achieve rapid growth without substantial capital imports.[34]
Nothing less than China's military security is seen to be
involved in the decision to propel a new "great leap forward" in the nation's economy that, according to Kang
Shih-en, minister of petroleum and chemical industries,
will certainly surpass that of 1958 in momentum, scale, and
scope.[35] As Chairman Hua put it to the national industrial
conference: "The question of the speed of construction is
a political rather than a purely economic question. When
viewed in the light of the international class struggle,
the political question stands out still more sharply. By
their very nature, imperialism and social-imperialism mean
war. We must definitely be ready for war. We cannot afford
to let time slip through our fingers, as it waits for no
one."[36]
     Of course, because China does not publish its economic
plans, we do not know what goals the Fifth Five-Year Plan
has set for oil production. Although one might have sus-
pected that these goals would be predicated on the 20 percent average annual growth rate that has given China pride
in its oil industry, they do not appear to be. When in
July 1977 the PRC issued the disappointing announcement
that crude oil output for the first six months of the year
"was over 10 percent higher than that of the same 1976
period," it claimed that "China fulfilled or overfulfilled
her January-June output plans for crude oil, natural
gas and petroleum products."[37] This may merely mean that
output plans were only temporarily scaled down for a brief
transitional period while the new leadership struggled to
overcome the problems created by the Gang of Four and a
fattening economy before moving production into high gear
again for the rest of the Fifth Five-Year Plan. But this
may reflect realistic recognition of the long-range obstacles to maintaining a 20 percent growth rate as production expands and as China's most accessible oil fields
become depleted. It may be that the degree of urgency
felt by the leadership is such that it is allocating an
even higher proportion of capital investment to oil

development than in the past. Some reports from Peking
suggest that the government now seeks drastically to go
beyond a 20 percent average annual increase in output,
which would be very hard to do.[38] Assuming that the present "moderate" leadership maintains both political stability and its current economic orientation and that no natural
disaster comparable to the Tangshan earthquake occurs, the
most that one can fairly project is that year-end production
figures for 1977 might show an increase comparable to last
year's 13 percent and that the average annual growth rate
might be 15 percent for the years 1978-80.

The problem of calculating the production base against
which these percentages are to be applied has been simpli-
fied by Peking's 1977 statements that crude oil output in
1976 was 7.7 times higher than in 1965.[39] Since 1965
output, formerly thought to have been 10 mmt, is now considered to have been roughly 11 mmt,[40] this means that 1976
production was approximately 84.7 mmt. That figure is lower
than we would have anticipated on the basis of our earlier
estimate of 1974 production and the subsequent remarks of
Chinese leaders to visiting foreign dignitaries,[41] but higher
than that assumed by the most pessimistic analysts.

If we apply our projected 13 percent growth rate for
1977 and 15 percent thereafter to the 84.7 mmt base, this
will lead to about a 145 mmt output in 1980. It should be
noted, however, that this newly confirmed 1976 base will
yield a 1980 output of over 165 mmt if the PRC can manage
a growth rate of 13 percent in 1977 and as much as 20 percent during the following three years as added investments
take effect.[42] If, on the other hand, a 10 percent average
annual growth rate is what takes place between now and 1980,
production that year will be only 124 mmt.

In any event, despite the recent decline in production
growth rates, the current leadership is doing its best to
convince the world that China's oil production is booming
in 1977, reporting the discovery of new high-yielding oilfields, the drilling of China's deepest well, progress in
offshore prospecting, and great advances in the laying of
oil pipelines.[43] Moreover, under the leadership of the
Taching Oil Refinery and seventeen other major refineries,
China's oil workers are being mobilized to take part in a
nationwide socialist labor emulation drive in which all
production units compete to increase their output.[44]
Oil is plainly expected to lead the way toward the economic
goal recently charted by Li Hsien-nien of "attaining great
order with initial 'success within this year and great
success in three years' time."[45]

Domestic Demand

The urgency of the PRC's need to increase oil production
becomes apparent when one considers its swiftly growing
domestic demand for energy as well as the desire of the
current leadership to expand oil exports. In 1975 we noted
that because China's economy has been essentially agricultural, it has been possible to meet most energy requirements
with coal.[46] We cited an apparently careful Japanese estimate that, as late as the early 1970s, the PRC was using
oil to meet only slightly over 10 percent of its needs, with
coal representing over 85 percent of energy consumption and
natural gas and hydroelectric power some 4 percent. We
emphasized, however, that although China's reliance on oil
was still relatively small compared with the United States'
44 percent and Japan's 73 percent, during the previous
decade it had increased two and one-half times and was sure
to grow rapidly in both relative and absolute terms as
primary energy demands multiplied. The key question, we
pointed out, is whether China's future energy needs will
absorb the anticipated substantial increases in oil production, leaving little oil to export.

To illustrate the seriousness of the situation, we
invoked the reasonable estimate of some observers that in
1980 primary energy demand might outstrip coal production
by over 300 mmt of coal equivalent, that petroleum, natural
gas, and hydroelectric power would be called upon to fill
the gap, and that 150 million tons of oil (one ton of oil
converts to roughly 1.5 tons of coal equivalent)[47] would
barely cover two-thirds of it. This calculation was based
on the assumptions that industrial output and coal production would continue to grow at cumulative annual rates of
10 percent and 7 percent respectively, creating by 1980 a
primary energy demand of some 890 million tons of coal
equivalent but only a coal supply of roughly 580 million
tons.

How does this assessment look two years later? The
work of other commentators makes it seem likely that, at
least by 1973, China had come to rely on oil for at least
15 percent of its energy demand rather than slightly over
10 percent, as the Japanese analysis on which we relied had
put it.[48] Although estimates vary, there is agreement that
oil's share of energy demand has continued to rise rapidly,
as we predicted it would. For example, one commentator
believes that in 1975 the PRC may have relied on oil to meet
as much as 20 percent of its needs and that by 1980 oil may
fill approximately one-third of energy consumption.[49]

But what will 1980 energy demand be? One calculation
puts it as low as 564 mmt of coal equivalent and anticipates
that oil would provide 33 percent, or 186 mmt, of coal
equivalent, which would equal 124 mmt of oil.[50] Another

estimate for 1980 takes 560 mmt of coal equivalent as a
lower limit and 690 as an upper limit.[51] If oil is called
upon to provide one-third of the higher figure, this will
require over 153 mmt of oil. Similarly, in late 1975 the
CIA estimated that the 1980 energy demand may be as high as
725 mmt of coal equivalent or as low as 616 mmt and that
oil's share may be as high as 35 percent or as low as 26
percent.[52] This figure of 35 percent of 725 mmt would
require a whopping 169 mmt of oil to meet 1980 energy
demand, whereas 26 percent would require only 126 mmt of
oil.
      Because of the recession that China entered in 1976,
1980 demand should not be as high as the 890 mmt of coal
equivalent we earlier thought plausible. Nevertheless,
it can be expected to reach the "high" 725 mmt anticipated
by the CIA. If so, as the above calculations suggest, the
crucial factor in determining the availability of oil for
export will be the precentage of that demand filled by oil.
If in 1980 it turns out to be 30 percent or more, all of
the output of 145 mmt that we project for China will be
taken up by domestic demand. If, on the other hand, it
should be roughly 25 percent, as our 1975 essay assumed and
as we continue to assume, that would require only 120 mmt of
oil, leaving some 25 mmt for possible export.
      Which of these broad, ball-park conjectures will prove
most accurate will depend upon many variables.[53] How fast
will the economy actually grow? To what extent will the
range of Chinese efforts to conserve energy prove successful? It will make an enormous difference whether in 1980
energy demand is 890 mmt of coal equivalent or merely 560
mmt. And to what extent will intense oil-using sectors of
the economy develop faster than other sectors? The three
principal oil consumers that we identified in 1975--agri-
culture, transportation, and defense--all have ambitious
plans for modernization that will make increasing claims
upon oil. The PRC has set itself the goal of "basically"
mechanizing agriculture by 1980.[54] The many improvements
scheduled in China's transportation networks will require
a greater supply of oil to sustain them, and they will
make oil more accessible to consuming enterprises. Peking
is also determined to acquire up-to-date military technology
in the near future,[55] as well as other oil-consuming industrial facilities.
      On the supply side, although natural gas output now
meets almost 10 percent of energy needs, when calculating
the demand for oil the major questions still concern coal.
How rapidly will coal production grow, and to what extent
will oil be permitted to displace coal in situations
where either can be used? For years coal was assigned
a lower priority than oil in the PRC's investment hierarchy,
and output dramatically rose and fell in response to

political and economic vicissitudes, even while production
compiled a long-run 7 percent annual growth rate. Coal
fared badly in 1974,[56] and this apparently stimulated
awareness of the need to allocate larger resources to the
industry. Consequently 1975 proved an especially good year
as production rose by over 10 percent to 430 mmt.[57] Then
the Tangshan earthquake of mid-1976 struck the Kailuan
coal mine "as if the mine had been ruined by war."[58] Yet,
despite this setback to China's biggest mine, which sacrificed perhaps one-third of its annual production of 27 mmt,
and despite the fact that 1976 was the economy's worst
year in a decade, nationwide coal production for the year
is thought to have reached roughly 450 mmt, a gain of some
4.6 percent over 1975.[59] Moreover, as its contribution to
the country's current emulation drive, Kailuan is striving
to regain its pre-earthquake production capacity by the
end of 1977.[60] The PRC is also pressing the search for
new coalfields and recently announced discovery of a large,
high-quality coal mine in Anhwei Province that will soon
provide a substantial boost to coal production.[61] And the
tremendous effort now being made to improve the railways,
which "had been the salient weak link in the national
economy due to the serious damage caused by the 'gang of
four'"[62] and which devote a large proportion of their
capacity to shipping coal,[63] should enhance coal's attrac-
tiveness to consumers.
     Plainly, if coal production can reach 590 mmt in 1980,
which it will if it can continue to register average annual growth of 7 percent, it will increase the likelihood
that there will be surplus oil production available for
export, even if energy needs should reach the high 725
mmt figure that we project. Of course, an insignificant
amount of coal is always allocated for export, and bumper
production in 1980 would enable the PRC to export somewhat
more coal as well as free more oil for export. A major question, however, is whether Peking will be willing to make
the investment in the coal industry required to sustain
rapid progress in the face of great obstacles. Competition
for resources is very keen among the sectors of China's
economy, and it is uncertain what priority will be assigned
to coal in comparison with oil, natural gas, hydroelectric
power, nuclear power, and other energy sources, as well as
in comparison with other aspects of the economy.
     In these circumstances, where the projections for
energy needs and for production of coal, oil, and other
resources are necessarily based on inadequate information,
and where political as well as economic imponderables and
unknowns abound, it is understandable that specialists
differ over the amount of oil that will be required by
domestic demand in 1980, not to mention the more distant
future. In April 1977 the CIA, implicitly revising its

earlier research on China and anticipating its June 1977
report, claimed that the reserve and production outlook
for oil "is much less favorable than it appeared a few
years ago"; and it predicted that because of the increase
in domestic demand resulting from economic growth and coal
production problems, China would not have more than 25 mmt
of oil available for export by 1980 and that by 1985 exports
would fall to virtually nothing.[64] An earlier study by the
U.S. Bureau of Mines estimated that the PRC would be able
to export 50 mmt per year in the early 1980s and 100 mmt
in 1985,[65] an appraisal that some government experts still
endorse. Professor Cheng Chu-yuan, an American academic
specialist, recently predicted that 1980 oil production
would be no more than 176 million tons but that domestic
oil demand would be 120 million tons, leaving 56 million
tons for export.[66]
     Our own view of this maddeningly uncertain business is
that we expect China to have approximately 25 mmt of oil
for export in 1980. Although, as we have said, we anticipate that total domestic energy demand will reach 725 mmt
of coal equivalent, we are more sanguine about high coal
production in 1980 than we previously were, because we
believe that Peking has belatedly decided that it would be
literally counterproductive to go on treating coal as a
stepchild. Thus, it seems entirely possible that coal production might be 590 mmt and natural gas production might
reach 110 mmt of coal equivalent. If we disregard insignificant energy sources and suppose that 10 mmt of coal and
a similar volume of natural gas are allocated for export,
that would in theory only require 30 mmt of oil (yielding
45 mmt of coal equivalent) to make up the remaining energy
needs. We say "in theory" because this would mean that
Peking would be looking to oil to furnish not 33 percent
of energy needs in 1980 but perhaps only a bit over 6 percent, in order to gain the benefits of oil exports.
     In reality, however, oil and other fuels are not
fungible, and we cannot assume that oil is a mere residual
that will only be required to fill whatever energy needs
coal and natural gas are insufficient in quantity to meet,
leaving the rest of oil output for export. There are obviously many needs that only oil can meet, and these are
increasing with modernization. Moreover, even if we assume
that the PRC will be prepared to forgo new facilities that
consume oil whenever similar facilities that consume other
fuels can be built, there is nevertheless a question of
the extent to which Peking will be willing to invest in
converting many existing facilities from oil to other
fuels. For these reasons China will find it difficult to
keep oil's share of energy demand below 30 percent. Yet
it will have to do so if it is to assure itself the exports essential to future import plans. We believe that

the PRC is unlikely to succeed in reducing oil's share
below 25 percent, which, if we take 725 mmt of coal
equivalent as total energy needs in 1980, would require
some 181 mmt of coal equivalent or roughly 120 mmt of oil.
This, together with some 5 mmt of hydroelectric power,
would bring domestic energy supply to 866 mmt of coal
equivalent (coal 580, gas 100, oil 181, and hydroelectri-
city 5), enough to meet anticipated demand and still allow
an overage of 141 mmt or more than 15 percent of total
energy production for handling losses and additions to
inventory,[67] and for a possibly large expansion of coal
exports.

Since we anticipated that 1980 oil output will be 145
mmt, this should leave approximately 25 mmt of oil available for export. But one can see how thin the PRC's mar-
gin of safety is to assure even this relatively modest amount.
Failure to maintain a 15 percent growth rate in oil output
after 1977 or to hold oil's share of energy to 25 percent or
to keep energy demand from soaring or to meet other challenges
can result in little or no oil exports.

When it comes to China, where literally anything can
happen, four years is a very long time, and nine years an
eternity. We therefore think it pointless to attempt a
precise forecast for 1985. Nevertheless, we do believe that
the PRC is unlikely to allocate investments in ways that will
deprive it of the benefits that even modest oil exports can
confer. The volume of exports in 1985 may not be any greater
than in 1980, and may even be smaller, but it seems too pessimistic to conclude, as the April 1977 CIA analysis does,
that China's capacity for oil exports will by then be
negligible.

Exports and Foreign Trade

As we pointed out in 1975, despite China's vaunted self-
reliance policy, during the first half of the 1970s its
foreign trade expanded impressively and played an increasingly important role in the nation's economic development.
Since that time, however, China's foreign trade has stag-
nated. The current leadership in Peking has blamed this
on the hostility of the Gang of Four to foreign trade
generally and to oil exports in particular. Mao's widow,
Chiang Ch'ing, and her comrades had charged that the Ministry of Foreign Trade had "unrestrainedly imported what
China can produce and limitlessly exported what is badly
needed at home."[68] Vice-Premier Chang Ch'un-ch'iao had
claimed: "We are exporting too many major items, a whole
bunch of things all at once," and he specifically lashed
out at imports of complete sets of equipments. Chiang
Ch'ing condemned the export of the PRC's oil and other

raw materials as "selling out its natural resources" and
declared that petroleum "is all being taken off to other
countries." She argued that "by exporting petroleum China
is shifting the international energy crisis on to the
Chinese people" and has saved the capitalist world from
its energy crisis. Moreover, even though "the decision to
export crude oil had been discussed and proposed by Premier
Chou En-lai and other leading comrades in the central
authorities and approved by Chairman Mao himself," the
Gang allegedly sabotaged the plan to export crude. According to the current attacks, "they clandestinely made trouble by directing their trusted followers in Shanghai and
Liaoning [Province] to willfully change many enterprises
fueled by coal to go over to petroleum. This greatly increased consumption of crude oil and upset the original
plan." As a result, "China's exports of crude were affected and its international prestige was impaired, resulting
in a bad influence politically and economically."

What these charges seek to explain is the fact that,
despite inflation, in 1975 China's foreign trade increased
by only 2.6 percent, reaching $14.3 billion ($6.96 billion
exports and $7.4 billion imports), and in 1976 it actually
suffered a decline from the preceding year for the first
time since the Cultural Revolution years of 1967-68.
Although 1976 exports were up 4 percent to $7.2 billion,
imports dropped by almost 15 percent.[69] Undoubtedly the
policies and practices of the Gang of Four had a significant impact on this adverse trend, as did the natural
disasters of 1976, the recession experienced by China's
principal trading partners, and other factors in addition to a shortage of foreign exchange. Yet the lack of
hard currency may persist as the most abiding constraint
upon imports long after the other factors have receded
into history.

Our 1975 essay emphasized that because of massive imports of plants, equipment, and technology from the West
and Japan in the early 1970s, for the first time in many
years China in 1974 registered a balance of payments deficit, one that may have run as high as $1.3 billion. We
pointed out that the PRC lacked the foreign exchange reserves to meet recurring deficits of that magnitude and
that if it intended to continue its program of capital
imports, it would have to borrow funds, reduce other
imports, or earn substantially more from exports.

What we witnessed during 1975 and 1976 was a great
Chinese effort to get back in the black by resorting to
all three options to varying extents and at the same time
sharply reducing the purchase of new plants and equipment
from abroad. While maintaining its long-standing refusal
to accept long-term foreign credits and foreign proposals
for joint ventures or other forms of equity investment,

the PRC has continued to accept short- and medium-term credits under various guises such as "deferred payments," "overdrafts," and "reciprocal deposits of currencies" between Chinese and foreign banks and to discuss other possibilities of financing that would not offend its self-reliance posture. Despite the difficult circumstances of the period, it also managed to boost exports by over 5 percent in 1975 and by roughly 4 percent in 1976.[70] And it held imports to a standstill in the former year, and as we have seen, reduced them by about 15 percent last year. These efforts reduced the PRC's trade deficit to $455 million in 1975 and brought about a $900 million surplus last year, leading at least one Japanese economist to conclude that "difficulties in the foreign exchange aspect have been largely dissolved."[71] That conclusion, however, seems too optimistic unless China is to abandon the program of massive capital imports that it is now preparing to renew. Moreover, the recent $700 million purchase of wheat from Canada and Australia[72] should remind us that in order to achieve its 1976 balance-of-payments surplus, China had to reduce the purchase of wheat and other nontechnological imports to levels that it could not indefinitely sustain. As we stated in 1975, "the PRC is bound to find it very painful to substantially reduce nontechnological imports."[73]

The bottom line remains today what it was two years ago. Unless China is prepared to soften its resistance to foreign loans or investments, a large increase in oil exports still seems necessary to finance its contemplated capital import program. How large is that program likely to be? To be sure, there are economic limits to China's ability efficiently to utilize new capital equipment and technology. Although the Gang of Four is overthrown, there are also ideological limits. Even moderate leaders have to worry about how much foreign influence the Chinese people can be exposed to without succumbing to the "silver-coated bullets of the bourgeoisie." Yet these constraints are unlikely to discourage the Hua Kuo-feng government from importing $2 billion to $3 billion of capital goods per year. During the two years beginning mid-1972 the PRC contracted for a total of $2.4 billion in complete plants alone.[74] In view of the overthrow of the Gang of Four, intervening inflation, the loss of over two years in ordering many new plants, and the ambitions of the present leaders, an estimate of $2 billion to $3 billion per year in new orders seems plausible.

Can the export of oil meet the bill, as we anticipated in 1975? Oil exports made the major contribution to PRC foreign exchange in 1975, increasing 73 percent over the previous year and accounting for virtually all of China's export growth that year. China sold a total of 10 mmt

of crude oil to Japan, the Philippines, Rumania, and North
Korea and 1.3 mmt of refined products to Hong Kong, Vietnam, Cambodia, Thailand, and Laos. This yielded some $910
million,[75] not a small figure to a country that ran a $455
million deficit that year and earned less than $7 billion
from all exports. Oil exports in 1976 were slightly lower
than in 1975, in part because of the interference of the
Gang of Four, who for a time managed to reduce oil shipments
to Japan and to suspend shipments to the Philippines,[76] and
because of the need to divert potential surplus to domestic
uses to replace coal production lost in the great earthquake. Nevertheless, the approximately $700 million earned
from these exports was indispensable to the PRC's achievement in registering a foreign exchange surplus of $900
million.
     To the extent that the PRC can substantially increase
oil exports between now and the 1980s, it will be able to
finance the large capital goods orders contemplated without
succumbing to the blandishments of foreign investors or
long-term lenders. For example, at the current price of
over $13 per barrel that Peking charges for most of its oil
(some is sold at a lower "friendship price"), if it could
manage to export 50 mmt of crude in 1980, it would earn
perhaps $4.5 billion. Most of this could be allocated to
new capital imports, and there would also be added earnings
from higher sales of refined products. If, as seems more
likely, China should manage to export only about 25 mmt of
crude in 1980--over twice as much as 1976--this would yield
well over $2 billion in foreign exchange and finance new
capital imports of only something over $1 billion. In the
latter case, unless Peking could be confident that oil
exports would rise more dramatically after 1980, it would
be confronted with the prospect of cutting back its capital
purchase plans once again or expanding its resort to borrowing under one guise or other.
     Yet, assuming that an oil surplus of 20 to 50 million
tons can be generated for export in 1980, will it be possible to sell that much Chinese oil? Did Chinese oil exports
slump in 1976 only because of factors on the Chinese side,
or was there a falling off of interest on the part of foreign purchasers? In 1975 we noted that despite the high
wax content of Chinese oil, Japan will be happy to absorb
much of what is available for export in the near future.
That statement still stands, although the intervening
experience of two years has illuminated the complexities
of the situation.
     Japan has been by far China's largest oil customer,
alone taking more than the entire amount imported by all
other countries together. In 1975 Japan vindicated our
expectation that it would that year double its 1974 purchases by importing over 8 mmt. But the prediction of

some Japanese petroleum experts, which we noted, that
China might supply as much as 18 mmt to Japan in 1976 fell
flat on its face. Chinese oil exports to Japan in 1976
fell to 6.15 mmt, for reasons that specialists have debated.
In early 1977, at the first meeting of the Japan-China Mixed
Committee on Trade after the downfall of the Gang of Four,
Chinese delegates explained that the overall drop in Sino-
Japanese trade, in which reduced oil exports figured pro-
minently, was a temporary phenomenon brought on by the
recession in Japan, the Tangshan earthquake and the economic distortions caused by the Gang of Four.[77]

Actually, however, the situation is more complex than
those remarks imply. The physical characteristics of
Chinese oil have proved more troublesome than foreign importers originally appreciated. As we pointed out in our
previous essay, unlike Middle Eastern oil, Chinese crude
is desirable to pollution-conscious countries because of
its low sulfur content, but its much higher wax content is a
serious defect, especially to countries such as Thailand
and the Philippines that lack Japan's large refining facilities. Chinese oil has also become notorious for having a
high "pour point," which is the temperature below which
the oil will not flow freely and will solidify in pipelines
or storage. For example, it often has a pour point of over
90 degrees Fahrenheit or even body temperature, compared
to 10 to 20 degrees for most Middle Eastern crude, and its
best temperature can be as high as 130 degrees. This
requires importers to keep it constantly heated, which is
not only a considerable burden but also dangerous because
the oil has a rather low "flash point," so that heating it
to a temperature that will enable it to flow easily increases
the risk of fire or explosion.[78] It also contains more water
and sediment than the oil of many other nations.

Even Japan has had greater difficulty than it anticipated in refining China's crude, and Japanese importers
have also been disturbed at how "heavy" Chinese oil is,
that is, how small a percentage of "light" oils it yields
in refining. Taching crude, upon which Japan has largely
relied to date, distills into less than 30 percent light
oils (petrol 10 percent in volume, kerosene 5.4 percent,
and gas 13.8 percent). This leaves 70 percent heavy oil,
for which Japan, in view of its traditional reliance on
Middle Eastern crude, with its higher percentage of light
derivatives, has less demand.[79] Because of these difficulties Japan has burned an increasing proportion of
Chinese crude as "raw fuel" for power companies and steel
plants. Since nearly 10 percent of the roughly 270 million tons of oil imported by Japan each year from all world
sources is consumed in this unrefined state, the relative
unsuitability of Chinese crude for refining purposes is
not an absolute bar to its purchase by Japan so long as the

volume of imports from China does not grow too large.
Nevertheless it does put Chinese oil at a competitive disadvantage, and the Japanese would like to refine a greater
percentage of Chinese oil rather than burn it "raw,"
which they consider relatively wasteful.[80]
    China has equipped its refineries to cope with the
special problems presented by its crude, and Japan can certainly do the same. The question for the Japanese, however,
is whether it is worth doing so. The construction of facilities to maintain high temperatures, to remove the wax at
an early stage of processing, and to maximize the yield of
light oils from China's crude will be very expensive.[81]
Japanese refiners claim that "to extract gasoline, kerosene,
and residuals from China's oil in the same proportion as
that from Middle Eastern oil, adds $2.00-$3.00 a barrel to
the price."[82] Although this claim may be somewhat exaggerated in the hope of persuading the Chinese to reduce the
price of their oil and thereby encourage Japanese purchasers, there is no doubt that adapting Japanese industry to
Chinese crude will require substantial capital outlays.
Private companies that have already invested large sums to
desulfurize Middle Eastern oil and that are still feeling
the effects of the energy crisis and recession are understandably reluctant to make such outlays, especially without assurance that China will provide a long-term, stable,
and significant supply of oil at a reasonable price. By
the end of 1975 it had become apparent that for these reasons Japanese importers of crude had refused to commit
themselves to purchase as much Chinese oil in 1976 as they
had in 1975 and were reluctant to go along with a contemplated Japanese government proposal to China for a five-
year agreement under which they would have had to import
10 mmt in 1977 and gradually increase the volume up to
15 mmt in 1980.
    For political and economic reasons the oil importers'
position troubled the Japanese government. It worried
about the dissatisfaction that Chinese officials expressed
with the new attitude of the previously eager Japanese
oil industry. It also recognized that this would set back
its efforts to diversify the sources of Japan's oil supply,
which remains overwhelmingly dependent on the Middle East.
And it was unhappy about the implications for Sino-Japanese
trade, which was already unbalanced in Japan's favor and
which would require greater Chinese oil exports to pay for
the increased steel and other products that Japan planned
to sell China. Thus, to benefit overall relations with
China, in mid-January 1976 a Japanese government-industry
trade mission visited China to present the proposal for the
five-year oil import agreement mentioned above. Political
conditions in China at that time precluded successful negotiations, however. As we have seen, China's 1976 oil

exports to Japan proved 25 percent lower than the previous
year's, and overall Sino-Japanese trade slumped for the
first time in eight years, Japan's imports going down by
over 10 percent and its exports to China dropping as much
as 26.4 percent.[83]
     By the spring of 1977 the newly consolidated Hua Kuo-
feng government seemed ready to negotiate a long-term arrangement with Japan, and a high-powered delegation from Japan's
most prestigious business organization, Keidanren, was de-
lighted to receive a Chinese proposal for a five- to ten-
year trade agreement under which China would sell oil and
coal to Japan, and Japan would sell China steel, other construction materials, and technology, including items required for the development of the oil and coal industries.
Chairman Hua himself met the delegation and put his blessing
on the arrangement, which the Japanese accepted in principle
and are now seeking to spell out. In view of the added
expense of refining Chinese oil, the Japanese are currently
attempting to convince the Chinese to reduce its price,
which was raised in 1976 to $13.15 per barrel, and Japanese
refiners, who do not want to be left holding the bag in an
unprofitable situation, are asking their government for
inexpensive official financing of the new facilities they
will need to process the Chinese oil.[84] As of mid-1977 the
PRC has not made any concessions on price, despite Japanese
claims that this would encourage purchases by Japan's oil
companies and finance an export boom from Japan to China.
Not surprisingly, Japan's imports of Chinese oil in 1977
are not expected to exceed 1976 figures.
     Nevertheless, the first signs have appeared that Japan's
oil industry and government are preparing to cooperate in
processing larger volumes of Chinese crude. Shortly after
the Keidanren mission concluded the long-term agreement with
Peking, a major Japanese refiner, Idemitsu Kosan Company,
announced plans to install special hydrocracking equipment
to convert the heavy Taching crude into light oils at a
new refinery. The special equipment, which will be completed in three years, will have a daily capacity of 70,000
barrels and is estimated to cost roughly $200 million.[85]
A month later, former minister of international trade and
industry, Toshio Komoto, now chairman of the ruling Liberal
Democratic party's Policy Affairs Research Council, stated
that in view of the pending long-term agreement, the government's fiscal 1978 budget would incorporate necessary measures to promote Sino-Japanese trade, perhaps including
subsidies for construction of facilities to refine Chinese
crude.[86]
     It is still too early in the current Sino-Japanese
negotiations to know how great the anticipated jump in PRC
oil sales to Japan will be. The previously mentioned
proposal to gradually increase exports to reach 15 mmt

in 1980 may be accepted. Though even lesser figures have
been mentioned, the latest reports from Tokyo suggest that
Japan is planning to offer to purchase as much as 30 mmt
from China in 1985. Given the preparations that the PRC
has been making in recent years by improving pipelines to
ports as well as ports themselves and by acquiring increased
numbers of tankers,[87] Peking seems to anticipate total oil
exports to Japan and other countries of at least 25 mmt
annually. Although China has not yet developed a port that
can handle the largest tankers, making the transport of its
oil relatively expensive, this is not expected to present a
serious problem unless annual crude exports reach the 25 to
50 mmt range.[88] In mid-1976 an American government specialist noted that existing crude transmission lines to port
already had a capacity in excess of 30 mmt a year. Moreover,
he saw substantial hopes for export not only in the extensive negotiations with Japan but also in PRC attempts to
market crude oil elsewhere in the world including Europe.[89]
In 1976 the PRC did sell crude to West Germany and possibly
to Italy, as well as to Rumania.[90]
     China can also be expected to increase sales of refined
oil products, which currently go only to a handful of countries. Indeed, one of the unspoken bargaining chips that
the PRC can exploit in its negotiations with Japan is the
possibility that if China has difficulty selling crude
abroad, it may decide to export greater amounts of the
more profitable refined products in lieu of crude,
especially in view of the problems that other countries
encounter with Chinese crude. The development of China's
refining facilities long failed to keep pace with the rapid
increase in oil production,[91] but in recent years Peking
has expanded them as part of a massive effort to build
petrochemical complexes near many major cities. The PRC
attempt to bring refining capacity into better balance
with crude production benefited from the latter's reduced
rate of growth in 1976, a reduction that reflected lower
expectations of oil exports to Japan as well as other factors.[92] To the extent that China can manage to produce
increasingly large quantities of refined products for
export as well as domestic consumption, it will be able
to enhance its foreign exchange earnings and free itself
of the need to rely on Japan and others to buy its crude.

                    Foreign Policy Implications

The upshot of our discussion is that China does not seem
destined to be an oil power in the sense of becoming one
of the world's leading oil exporters. If in 1980 it man-
ages to export 25 mmt, that would place it only thirteenth
among the oil exporting nations, according to their current

achievements. Every member of OPEC exports a larger
annual volume than that. Even if the PRC should be able
to export 50 mmt, it would rank only tenth if present
figures are maintained by other exporters.
    Nor is it probable that oil exports of 20 to 50 mmt
will add significantly to Peking's importance in an absolute
sense. Even if China were to be able to sell Japan 40 mmt
in 1980, that would only meet roughly 15 percent of Japan's
anticipated oil needs, and the PRC will probably have less
than half that quantity available for export to Japan. A
fortiori, the United States, Western Europe, and other oil
importers are unlikely to find China offering them a substantial new source of supply. The major Western oil companies that dominate the marketing of the world's oil need
not fear that the PRC, by excluding them from participation
in its oil development, will independently market a large
volume of oil through channels outside their control and
thereby threaten their domination.
    Because the PRC will only be expanding oil exports
to a modest extent, it can be expected to seek new techniques for financing desired capital imports without
appearing to compromise its cherished self-reliance policy.
A recent tour of European financial centers by a high-rank-
ing delegation from the Bank of China and a visit to China
by top Japanese bankers fueled speculation that China may
be willing to assume long-term foreign debt without calling
it such. Certainly the Chinese are showing interest in
acquiring easier terms on deferred payments for imports.
It is even possible that Peking may decide to join the
International Monetary Fund and perhaps other multilateral
financial organizations in order to enhance its access to
foreign financing.[93]
    China's failure to become a major oil exporter should
not obscure the fact that it has already become an oil
power in a more limited but very important sense. It
imports only a fraction of what it exports and is self-
sufficient in oil and likely to remain so if it continues
to give high priority to the discovery, extraction, and
refining of its crude reserves both offshore and onshore.
By the mid-1980s it may be the only major industrial country able to sustain economic development without relying
upon other nations' oil. Some experts predict that by
1985 even the Soviet Union, now the world's leading oil
producer and the third-ranking exporter, may join the
Western industrial powers and Japan in having to compete
for OPEC's dwindling oil for its own use.[94] Whether or
not that prediction proves accurate, China promises to be
in an advantageous position, relatively independent of
external suppliers at least until it reaches an advanced
state of industrialization.
    By not becoming a major oil exporter the PRC avoids

certain diplomatic problems. Reduced prospects for Chinese
exports to Japan will diminish Soviet anxieties about the
development of intimate Sino-Japanese contacts. Moreover,
by not exporting large quantities Peking will avoid the
political strains that would come from unregulated competition with the Middle Eastern states and other OPEC members. It will feel under little pressure to join OPEC,
membership in which subjects countries to various political
and economic constraints. For example, this will leave
China free to continue charging cut-rate "friendship
prices" for oil to specially favored customers rather than
adhere to OPEC prices. Usually these low prices involve
such small quantities as to preclude antagonizing other
exporters. Although PRC exports are thus far nowhere near
the level of worrying the Arab states, Indonesia has already
come to feel Chinese competition for the Japanese market.
In 1974 Indonesia sold Japan more than eight times as much
crude as did China, but in 1975 and 1976 only slightly more
than three times as much.[95] Indonesia's vulnerability can
be seen from the fact that it relies on oil exports for
57 percent of domestic revenue and 46 percent of net
foreign exchange earnings and that Japan buys over 45 percent of Indonesia's crude.[96] If China substantially
increased its export of crude to Japan while continuing
to charge Japan less than Indonesia does, it could quite
seriously affect Indonesia's oil income. The currently
anticipated growth of China's crude exports to Japan,
while a source of concern to Indonesia, is unlikely to be
large enough to add significantly to the tensions that
mark the long-troubled Peking-Jakarta relationship.
     What the PRC will be forgoing, however, is the ability
to use oil as a highly influential political weapon. For
example, the possibility mentioned in our 1975 essay--that
China might some day export so much oil to Japan as to gain
undue leverage over it--is not going to be realized. This
does not mean, of course, that Peking will not be able to
extract some mileage from even the modest amount of oil
export contemplated under the agreement currently being
negotiated with Japan. Indeed, by skillfully exploiting
the thirst for oil of Japan's business community, Peking
persuaded Keidanren, the influential private organization
that opened the negotiations in Tokyo's behalf in 1977,
to advocate for the first time early conclusion of the
long-awaited Japan-China peace and friendship treaty,
including the controversial antihegemony clause that is
anathema to the USSR.[97] Nevertheless, such minor diplomatic achievements do not require the kind of political
leverage necessary to prevent Japan from cooperating with
the USSR in a variety of programs designed to develop,
and to permit Japan to share in, Soviet energy resources.
     Yet nothing less than that was the PRC goal in the

palmy days of 1974-75 when Tokyo was rife with expectations
of prodigious Chinese oil exports. Those expectations
actually played an important role in dulling Tokyo's enthusiasm for the projects that Moscow dangled before it.
Similarly, the need for Japan to ratify the January 1974
Japan-South Korea agreement to develop jointly the oil
potential of the disputed continental shelf seemed less
pressing if China could soon be counted on for 50 to 100
mmt of crude each year. Once that bubble burst, Japan
had to renew its search for other sources of oil that
promised relief from its extreme reliance upon OPEC and
particularly Middle Eastern crude, just as in 1975 we predicted it would if China failed to fulfill the expectations
it had encouraged. Consequently, although Japan's relations with both the USSR and South Korea have been marred
by political tensions, the Japanese have felt obliged to
follow up on plans to cooperate with those countries in
producing energy.
     This has contributed to the recent cooling of Sino-
Japanese relations. Despite the evolving arrangement for
expansion of Chinese crude exports to Japan, increasing numbers of Japanese have come to perceive China not so much
as assisting Japan in its search for alternative energy
sources as hindering it. Not only has the PRC continued to
mobilize political pressure to discourage Japan's participation in Soviet energy schemes, but it has also sharpened
its attacks upon the South Korea-Japan undersea oil extraction
agreement, which was recently revived by the Diet's belated
approval. As pressure for Diet approval mounted, Peking
issued a series of warnings reiterating the PRC's position
that the bilateral agreement for a "Joint Development Zone"
on the continental shelf in the East China Sea is an unacceptable infringement on Chinese sovereignty that seeks to
present the PRC with a fait accompli by dividing the continental shelf without consulting it.[98] The Japanese government reacted calmly to China's protests, maintaining that
the agreement in no way infringed Peking's rights over the
shelf, that Japan was prepared to negotiate shelf demarcation with Peking, that the PRC was merely stating its view
for the official record, and that approval of the agreement would not harm Sino-Japanese relations.[99] China's
response to Diet approval was a "serious protest" issued
by its Foreign Ministry, which stated in part:

          The East China Sea continental shelf is the
          natural extension of the Chinese continental
          territory. The People's Republic of China has
          inviolable sovereignty over the East China Sea
          continental shelf. It stands to reason that the
          question of how to divide those parts of the East
          China Sea continental shelf which involve other

countries should be decided by China and the countries
concerned through consultations. The so-called Japan-
South Korea agreement on joint development of the
continental shelf signed by the Japanese government
with the South Korean authorities unilaterally behind
China's back is entirely illegal and null and void.
Without the consent of the Chinese government, no
country or private person may undertake development
activities on the East China Sea continental shelf.
Whoever does so must bear full responsibility for
all the consequences arising therefrom.[100]

By invoking the international law theory, long held by the
PRC, that the continental shelf is the natural extension of
Chinese territory and therefore presumptively belongs to
China, the Foreign Ministry implicitly repudiated Japan's
assumption that the allocation of rights over the continental
shelf will eventually be decided according to the median
line theory. According to this theory, when countries
separated by water are geographically too close to permit
each to proclaim an exclusive 200-mile economic zone offshore, their economic zones are bounded by drawing a line
equidistant from the opposing coastlines, thus allocating
resources according to the geographical characteristics of
the surface rather than the seabed. As so often occurs
with Chinese views of international law, the People's Daily
then made explicit what the government had left implicit.
In an article signed by "Commentator," the nom de plume of
a high official, it stated:

> It is known to all that the East China Sea continental
> shelf is the natural extension of the Chinese conti-
> nental territory and forms an integral part of the
> mainland. Our country has inviolable sovereignty
> over the East China Sea continental shelf. Certain
> members of the Japanese government circles even
> alleged that "the Japan-South Korea joint development
> zone is restricted to the Japanese side of the inter-
> mediate line of equal distance between Japan and
> China," and does not infringe on China's sovereignty.
> Such argument is futile and utterly untenable. The
> Chinese government and people will absolutely not
> tolerate any activity violating China's sovereignty
> and deliberately trampling on the norms of inter-
> national law.[101]

Whether or not Peking's view of the relevant international law will actually be endorsed by the ongoing United
Nations Law of the Sea Conference and applied to the circumstances of East Asia, it plainly has an immediately
chilling effect on plans to move ahead with the Japan-South
Korea agreement. Chinese Deputy Premier Li Hsien-nien

recently criticized the Japanese government for taking
the PRC's protests too lightly,[102] and respect for Peking's
position is sure to be reflected in opposition in the Diet
to legislation required to implement the agreement.

South Korean leaders, of course, continue to feel
extremely frustrated by China's attitude toward their determined effort to develop their own oil resources. Although
in principle Peking claims that shelf demarcation should be
decided by the countries concerned through consultations,
it refuses to respond to the South Korean government's
offers to consult with it. Peking's view is that it will
only consult what it deems to be the sole legitimate government of Korea, that of Kim Il Sung. Chinese officials say
that once Korea is unified under a legitimate regime,
there will be no difficulty in resolving the matter of
shelf boundaries and that unification can promptly take
place after the complete withdrawal of American forces from
the peninsula.

Because of the two-Korea problem and China's opposition, Japan is unlikely to regard the Japan-South Korea
agreement as opening up a new source of oil in the foreseeable future, even though Nippon Oil Company of Japan plans
to begin joint venture exploration under the agreement,
together with Korean and American companies.[103] We should
therefore expect further Japanese efforts to develop undersea oil without the participation of South Korea in areas
of the continental shelf that are outside the bounds of
Korean claims. Japan may decide, for example, that it
will be more promising to open up bilateral negotiations
with China to permit joint exploitation of the presumably
oil-rich shelf area near the disputed Senkaku (Tiao-yu
tai) islands, even if it should prove impossible to resolve
the conflicting claims to the islands themselves. Yet this
would further complicate Japan's relations with the Republic of China on Taiwan, which also claims these islands.

Of course, so long as the ROC maintains a separate
existence from the PRC, lays claim to the Tiao-yu tai,
occupies some South China Sea islets and claims others,
and seeks to exploit offshore oil on the shelf it shares
with the mainland, there will also be a continuing possibility of conflict between Peking and Taipei over oil as
well as other matters. Here, as in the two-Korea situation,
Peking is patiently awaiting reunification of the country,
but that does not mean that it is necessarily prepared to
tolerate oil development by what it deems to be the ille-
gitimate government. Thus, American oil companies that
have leased oil development concessions from Taiwan have
to be at least as sensitive to China's attitude as those
that have similar arrangements with countries including
Japan and Korea and several in Southeast Asia whose claims
overlap China's.[104]

On balance, China's oil policy vis à vis some of the
Southeast Asian countries may present more problems than
solutions. Peking's ability to export relatively modest
amounts of oil to the Philippines and Thailand will deny
it some additional political influence in those nations.
At the same time China's gradually increasing interest in
developing offshore oil resources in the South China Sea
is likely to intensify its smoldering territorial disputes
with Vietnam and the Philippines over various islet group-
ings, especially the Paracels and the Spratlies,[105] and
over demarcation of sea and shelf boundaries.
    The PRC will undoubtedly deal with the range of thorny
island disputes and sea boundary problems within the context
of its overall political and economic objectives. In view
of its understandable preoccupation with the expanding
power of the Soviet Union and its desire to mobilize a
broad coalition of countries to contain Soviet advances in
Asia as well as elsewhere and to cooperate in the modernization of China, it is likely to seek reasonable solutions
through negotiations with all governments that it regards
as legitimate and that do not assume a pro-Soviet or anti-
Chinese posture. Given the worldwide quest for oil and the
nationalistic sensitivities of the countries involved,
Peking is well aware that if the complex territorial
problems that it confronts are mishandled, its coalition-
building effort might well founder. Yet the solutions
reached will have to take account of Peking's own nationalistic sensitivity and burgeoning need for oil as well as
the lengthening shadow that a stronger China will cast
over Asia.

Notes

    1. Chou En-lai, "Report on the Work of the Govern-
ment," Jan. 13, 1975, in The Fourth National People's
Congress (Hsinhua News Agency, Special Issue, Jan. 22,
1975), pp. 17-22.
    2. Choon-ho Park and Jerome Alan Cohen, "The Politics
of China's Oil Weapon," Foreign Policy no. 20 (Fall 1975):
28-49.
    3. See text at notes 14 and 15 infra and sources
cited therein; see also noted 10 infra.
    4. Ruth Youngblood, "China Lifting Cultural Bans"
(UPI, Hong Kong), Korea Herald (Seoul), June 1, 1977, p. 4.
    5. "Peking Said Drilling in South China Sea" (AFP,
Hong Kong), Mainichi Daily News (Tokyo), June 2, 1977,
p. 6; Chiang Shan-hao, "Taching Impressions," Peking Review,
no. 19 (May 6, 1977): 40-45, no. 20 (May 13, 1977): 25-29,
no. 21 (May 20, 1977): 20-24, and no. 22 (May 27, 1977):
24-27, 29.

6. See, e.g., "China Announces Gas Discoveries" (AFP, Hong Kong), Mainichi Daily News, June 1, 1977, p. 6.

7. "Peking Said Drilling in South China Sea"; "China's Oil--Recent Advances," Sino-British Trade, April 1976, p. 1.

8. Susumu Awanohara, "Warm Welcome in Peking," Far Eastern Economic Review, April 15, 1977, pp. 50-51.

9. Lee Lescaze, "Chinese May Import U.S. Oil Rigs," Washington Post, May 28, 1977, p. 14.

10. "Chairman Hua Kuo-feng's Speech at the National Conference on Learning from Taching in Industry," May 9, 1977, Peking Review, no. 21 (May 20, 1977): 7, 11-12.

11. Chou En-lai, p. 19.

12. Jen-min jih-pao [People's Daily] (Peking), May 11, 1977, pp. 1-2; see also "China Boasts of Ability to Pass U.S. in Oil Output" (AFP, Hong Kong), Mainichi Daily News, May 11, 1977, p. 6.

13. U.S. Central Intelligence Agency, China: Oil Production Prospects, June 1977, pp. 5-6.

14. See note 12 supra.

15. Yu Ch'iu-li, "Mobilize the Whole Party and the Nation's Working Class and Strive to Build Taching-Type Enterprises throughout the Country," May 4, 1977, Peking Review, no. 22 (May 27, 1977): 5, 17.

16. Rene Flipo, "Oil to Fuel China's New Leap" (AFP, Peking), Korea Herald, May 13, 1977, p. 4.

17. Some reports have given 24 mmt as Taching's 1976 output. See ibid., and Ross Munro, "Production of China's Oilfield at Taching May Have Peaked," New York Times, Dec. 27, 1976, p. D2. But United States government experts have estimated it at 38 mmt, and they note that some estimates put it as high as 43 mmt. See "PRC Petroleum Industry in 1976," MS available at U.S. Department of Commerce, p. 2.

18. Jen-min jih-pao, May 11, 1977, pp. 1-2.

19. Edward K. Delong, "Estimates of U.S. Oil Cut in Half," Washington Post, June 20, 1975, p. 1.

20. See, e.g., Choon-ho Park, "Oil under Troubled Waters: The Northeast Asia Sea-Bed Controversy," Harvard International Law Journal 14 (Spring 1973): 218-48, 257-60, and "The Sino-Japanese-Korean Sea Resources Controversy and the Hypothesis of a 200-Mile Economic Zone," Harvard International Law Journal 16 (Winter 1975): 33-38, 40-46. On current seabed oil explorations off the coasts of Japan, South Korea, Taiwan, and other East Asian countries, see Petroleum News: Southeast Asia (Hong Kong), Jan. 1977, pp. 28-29 (Japan), pp. 30-33 (Malaysia), pp. 37-40 (the Philippines), p. 41 (South Korea), p. 14 (Taiwan), and pp. 46-47 (Vietnam).

21. China: Oil Production Prospects, pp. 7-8. See

135   China's Oil Policy

also, e.g., Chu-yuan Cheng, "China's Future as an Oil
Exporter," New York Times, April 4, 1976, p. 2, who
writes: "Although based on scattered and fragmentary evidence, the conclusion of most experts is that China's oil
reserves, including the most recent discoveries, total
perhaps 220 billion barrels, of which only 22 billion
barrels can be counted as probable recoverable reserves
that would amount to only 3.8 percent of the world's proven
reserves as of 1974." For differing views, compare, e.g.,
K. P. Wang, The People's Republic of China: A New Industrial Power with a Strong Mineral Base (Washington, D.C.:
U.S. Bureau of Mines, 1975), pp. 29-30, with Tatsu Kambara,
"The Petroleum Industry in China," China Quarterly, no. 60
(Dec. 1974): 709-11.
     22. China: Oil Production Prospects, p. 22.
     23. Park and Cohen, "The Politics of China's Oil
Weapon," p. 33.
     24. See, e.g., Ho P'ing-ti, "China's Reserves Loom
Large on World Stage: Huge Oil Deposits Could Weaken Arab
Dominance," Los Angeles Times, Oct. 13, 1973, 1974, pt.
6, p. 1 ("400 mmt by 1980"); Ho's own Chinese version in
detail, "Chung-kuo shih shih-yu tze-yüan tsui feng-fu-ti
kuo-chia" [China is the country with the richest oil
resources], Ch'i-shih nien'tai [The Seventies] (Hong
Kong), Feb. 1975, pp. 6-14.
     25. Kambara, p. 717 ("153 mmt in 1980"); Chu-yuan
Cheng, China's Petroleum Industry: Output and Export
Potential (New York: Praeger, 1976), p. 40 ("176 mmt in
1980"); and U.S. Central Intelligence Agency, China:
Energy Balance Projections, Nov. 1975, pp. 12-13, 28-29
("medium" estimate of roughly 150 mmt considered reason-
able, and "high" estimate of some 196 mmt deemed unlikely).
     26. Fox Butterfield, "China Emerging as an Oil
Power," New York Times, Jan. 25, 1976, p. 38.
     27. See, e.g., Fang Hai, "P'i-p'an yang-nu che-hsüeh"
[Criticize the slavish comprador philosophy], Hung ch'i
[Red Flag], April 1976, pp. 21-26 (English translation in
Selections from PRC Magazines, April 1976, nos. 867-68,
pp. 22-23), in which Teng Hsiao-p'ing, "that unrepentant
capitalist roader within the Party," was condemned for
advocating a more vigorous export policy in order to
accelerate the exploitation of natural resources, quicken
the transformation of industry, and hasten the pace of
scientific research. This was labeled exchanging exports
for imports "in an unprincipled manner," a practice that
allegedly would "give to others the sovereign right to
open up mineral resources" and would turn China "into a
market where the imperialist countries dump their goods,
a raw material base, a repair and assembly workshop, and
an investment center."
     28. "Kuan-yü chia-k'uai kung-yeh fa-chan ti jo-kan

wen-t'i" [Certain questions concerning the acceleration of industrial development], Hsüeh-hsi yü p'i-p'an [Study and Criticism], April 1976, pp. 28-35 (English translation in Selections from PRC Magazines, June 1976, no. 873, pp. 4-6).
    29. Fang Hai.
    30. Peter Weintraub, "China Growth Slumps," Far Eastern Economic Review, March 11, 1977, p. 34.
    31. Ibid. Some U.S. government specialists believe that China probably experienced no growth in either GNP or industrial production in 1976.
    32. See, e.g., Kuo Chi, "Foreign Trade: Why the 'Gang of Four' Created Confusion," Peking Review, no. 9 (Feb. 25, 1977): 16-18.
    33. Fox Butterfield, "China Sets New Date for 5th 5-Year Plan," New York Times, Oct. 28, 1976, p. 10.
    34. Peter Weintraub, "Taching's Theme Is Growth," Far Eastern Economic Review, May 6, 1977, p. 51.
    35. Jen-min jih-pao, May 11, 1977, pp. 1-2.
    36. "Chairman Hua Kuo-feng's Speech," p. 13.
    37. "PRC Scores Record Output in Petroleum Industry," Peking, NCNA-English, July 12, 1977, reprinted in Foreign Broadcast Information Service (FBIS), Daily Report: People's Republic of China, July 13, 1977, p. E16.
    38. See, e.g., Flipo.
    39. "Closely Follow Chairman Hua, Propel the Movement for Industry to Study Taching to a New Stage," Jen-min jih-pao, May 4, 1977, p. 3, English translation in "27 April-3 May Taching Conference Activities Noted," FBIS, Daily Report: People's Republic of China, May 4, 1977, p. E1; see also "Spring Trade Fair Reflects Progress in Various Fields," ibid., May 16, 1977, p. E21 ("nearly 7.7 times higher than in 1965").
    40. China: Energy Balance Projections, p. 29, gives 10.8 mmt as its 1965 figure.
    41. In November 1975 Vice-Premier Li Hsien-nien reportedly told Japan's minister of international trade and industry, Toshio Komoto, that in 1975 China would produce close to 80 mmt. (Nihon Keizai Shinbun [Japan Economic Newspaper, Tokyo], Nov. 18, 1975, morning ed., p. 4; and Nihon Enerugi Keizai Kenkyusho [Japan Energy Economy Institute, Tokyo] Chugoku Sekyusangyono Genjo [Current status of China's oil industry], May 1976, p. 10); 13 percent of that figure would put 1976 output at about 90 mmt. In May 1976 Foreign Trade Minister Li Chiang reportedly told the late British foreign secretary, Anthony Crosland, that oil production was getting close to 100 mmt a year, as it would have if the PRC had sustained its growth rate of 20 percent in 1976 ("China's Oil--Recent Advances").
    42. See, e.g., China: Energy Balance Projections, pp. 13, 28, for the view that a 20 percent growth rate

is too high to expect in the period prior to 1980 and
15 percent more realistic.
    43. "China Puts High-Yielding Oil Field into Produc-
tion," Mainichi Daily News, Jan. 5, 1977, p. 6.
    44. Chou Chin, "Socialist Labor Emulation Drive on
the Upswing," Peking Review, no. 23 (June 3, 1977): 23, 25.
    45. Jen-min jih-pao April 9, 1977, p. 2.
    46. Park and Cohen, "The Politics of China's Oil
Weapon," p. 37.
    47. China: Energy Balance Projections, p. 14.
    48. See, e.g., Kokusai Boeki [International Trade]
(Tokyo), May 1, 1973, p. 3; Kambara, p. 716; Vaclav Smil,
"Energy in China: Achievements and Prospects," China
Quarterly, no. 65 (March 1976): 57; Cheng, p. 209; Bobby A.
Williams, "The Chinese Petroleum Industry: Growth and
Prospects," in China: A Reassessment of the Economy,
Joint Economic Committee, U.S. Congress (Washington, D.C.:
U.S. Government Printing Office, 1976), pp. 241-45; and
the CIA's China: Energy Balance Projections, p. 6.
Estimates of the share of oil in China's energy supply
pattern considerably vary. For 1970, Kokusai Boeki places
it at 10.5%, Smil at 9.7%, Williams at 11.34%, and the CIA
at 14%. For 1973, Cheng and Kambara both place it at 15%.
For 1974, Williams places it at 17.01% and the CIA at 22%.
    49. Kambara, p. 716.
    50. Ibid.
    51. Smil, p. 81.
    52. China: Energy Balance Projections, pp. 11-12.
    53. For the most sophisticated discussion of these
variables, see ibid. generally.
    54. "Fundamental Way Out for Agriculture Lies in
Mechanization," in Hsinhua Weekly (Hong Kong), Dec. 25,
1976, pp. 20-22 (the English version of an editorial in
Jen-min jih-pao, Dec. 23, 1976).
    55. See, e.g., Jerome Alan Cohen, "A China Policy for
the Next Administration," Foreign Affairs 55 (Oct. 1976):
20, 21-25; Michael Pillsbury, "US-China Military Ties?"
Foreign Policy, no. 20 (Fall 1975): 50-57; and Drew
Middleton, "What the Chinese Forces Lack: Most Types of
Modern Weapons," New York Times, June 24, 1977, p. A3.
    56. See China: Energy Balance Projections, p. 3.
    57. See, e.g., "PRC Coal Industry: Performance and
Prospects" (The Editor), Current Scene, May 1976, p. 14;
and "China Economic Notes," in U.S.-China Trade Review,
Sept.-Oct. 1976, p. 54.
    58. "Kailan Coal Mines Speeds Up Restoration of Pro-
duction," Peking Review, no. 13 (March 25, 1977): 6.
    59. Weintraub, "China Growth Slumps."
    60. Chou Chin, p. 24.
    61. "China Reveals Discovery of Coal Mine in Anhwei"
(AFP Hong Kong), Mainichi Daily News, March 30, 1977,

p. 6; "New Coalfield," Peking Review, no. 21 (May 20, 1977): 32.
        62.   "Railway Transport Turns for the Better," Peking Review, no. 13 (March 25, 1977): 5.
        63.   Chou Chin, p. 23.
        64.   U.S. Central Intelligence Agency, The International Energy Situation: Outlook to 1985, April 1977, p. 13.
        65.   Wang, p. 38.
        66.   "China's Trade Not Expected to Rise" (AFP, Taipei), Mainichi Daily News, April 20, 1977, p. 6.
        67.   In calculating energy supply for 1980, the CIA assumes that 8% of that year's total energy production should be allocated to "handling losses, additions to inventory, and a small amount of petroleum consumed by the military" and should therefore not be included in supply. (China: Energy Balance Projections, p. 29). Our estimates for both supply and demand do not separate military uses from other needs.
        68.   The quotations in this paragraph are all from Kuo Chi, pp. 16-17.
        69.   Satoshi Imai, "China's External Trade Continuing Adjustment," JETRO China Newsletter, April 1977, p. 1.
        70.   The figures in this paragraph are from ibid., p. 5.
        71.   Ibid., p. 17.
        72.   Fox Butterfield, "The Chinese Economy Is Playing Catch-Up," New York Times, June 12, 1977, pt. 4, p. 4.
        73.   Park and Cohen, "The Politics of China's Oil Weapon," p. 42.
        74.   Imai, p. 9.
        75.   U.S. Central Intelligence Agency, People's Republic of China: International Trade Handbook, Oct. 1976, p. 3.
        76.   See Imai, p. 13.
        77.   "Group Confident about China Trade," Mainichi Daily News, March 4, 1977, p. 5.
        78.   David A. Andelman, "Thais Reject Chinese Oil As Too Waxy to Refine," New York Times, Sept. 19, 1975, p. 3.
        79.   Susumu Awanohara, "Snags Facing China's Oil Exports," Far Eastern Economic Review, Nov. 27, 1975, pp. 42, 47.
        80.   Ibid.
        81.   Ibid.
        82.   Alistair Wrightman, "Japan and China's Oil-- Proceeding with Caution," U.S.-China Business Review, March-April 1976, p. 34.
        83.   Awanohara, "Warm Welcome in Peking," p. 51.
        84.   Ibid.; Kokusai Boeki, Feb. 8, 1977, p. 1.
        85.   "Japan Oil Firm to Build Refinery for China Crude," Mainichi Daily News, April 3, 1977, p. 5.
        86.   "LDP on Cooperation with S.E. Asia, Trade with PRC," FBIS, Daily Report: Japan, May 20, 1977, p. C7.

        87.   "PRC Petroleum Industry in 1976," pp. 1, 6-7;
and "China's Tanker Fleet Growing," China Trade Report,
January 1977, pp. 6, 7.
        88.   "PRC Petroleum Industry in 1976," p. 7.
        89.   William Clarke, Director, Division of PRC Affairs,
U.S. Department of Commerce, "China's Economy," in National
Council for U.S.-China Trade, Speeches from the Conference
on China's Petroleum Industry, June 23, 1976, p. 17.
        90.   "PRC Petroleum Industry in 1976," p. 7.
        91.   A former employee of the PRC's oil industry who
is now in Hong Kong has written that certain aspects of the
country's oil-refining technology have reached the level
attained by the West in the 1960s but that in more crucial
respects the level is still not far above that of the West
in the 1950s (Huang Chung-te, "Chung-kuo shih-yu kung-yeh
kai-k'uang" [A summary of China's oil industry], Ch'i-shih
nien-tai, May 1977, pp. 7, 9-10).
        92.   Ibid., pp. 2, 4.
        93.   See Eric Morgenthaler, "Bankers from China
Touring Europe's Financial Centers," Wall Street Journal,
June 15, 1977, p. 16; Susumu Awanohara, "China Looks for
More Credit," Far Eastern Economic Review, May 27, 1977,
p. 78; "Second Thoughts," Far Eastern Economic Review,
June 24, 1977, p. 5. For an excellent analysis of the
PRC's position on foreign financing, see David L. Denny and
Frederic M. Surls, "China's Foreign Financial Liabilities,"
China Business Review, March-April 1977, pp. 13-21.
        94.   See the CIA's prediction to this effect in The
International Energy Situation: Outlook to 1985, pp. 12-13.
But see also Theodore Shabad, "West the Top Buyer of
Soviet Oil in '76," New York Times, June 11, 1977, p. 1,
27, who points to evidence suggesting that the USSR will
continue to respond to increased oil prices by adjusting
its fuel policies and consumption patterns to allow it
to maintain the large volume of oil exports that has
recently been providing 40% of its hard currency earnings.
        95.   Nihon Keizai Shinbun, March 26, 1977, morning
ed., p. 6; Robert F. Ichord, Jr., Energy Policies of the
World: Indonesia (Wilmington: Center for the Study of
Marine Policy, Univ. of Delaware, 1976), p. 41.
        96.   Guy Sacerdoti, "Wijarso Faces Up to the Oil Ghost,"
Far Eastern Economic Review, June 10, 1977, p. 43; and note
95 supra.
        97.   Awanohara, "Warm Welcome in Peking."
        98.   "Reiterating China's Stand on 'Japan-South Korea
Agreement for Joint Development of the Continental Shelf,'"
Peking Review, no. 23 (June 3, 1977): 7.
        99.   "China Protests Japan Bid to Ratify ROK Shelf
Pact," Japan Times (Kyodo, Peking), May 29, 1977, p. 3;
"China Informed of Shelf Pact Approval," ibid., June 10,
1977, p. 3.

100. "Statement by the Ministry of Foreign Affairs,"
June 13, 1977, Peking Review, no. 25 (June 17, 1977):
16, 17.
        101. Commentator, "China's Sovereignty over the Con-
tinental Shelf Brooks No Violation," Jen-min jih-pao,
June 14, 1977, p. 4 (partial English translation in
Peking Review, no. 25 [June 17, 1977]: 17).
        102. Kenji Nakano, "Li Discontent over Delay of Peace
Pact," Mainichi Daily News, June 27, 1977, p. 1.
        103. "Nippon Oil to Start Joint Shelf Venture,"
Mainichi Daily News, June 30, 1977, p. 5.
        104. For detailed discussion of the complex political
problems relating to China and offshore oil, see, e.g.,
Selig Harrison, "Time Bomb in East Asia," Foreign Policy,
no. 20 (Fall 1975): 3-27. For the legal background, see
Choon-ho Park, "Oil under Troubled Waters."
        105. For discussion of the legal aspects of this
problem, see Hungdah Chiu and Choon-ho Park, "Legal Status
of the Paracel and Spratly Islands," Ocean Development and
International Law 3, no. 1 (1975): 1-28.

7. The International Impact of China's Foreign Trade

Ralph N. Clough

China's enormous size creates a distinctive aura about the country which tends to distort the view of outside observers. It is difficult to place the activities of the Chinese in the proper perspective. For generations writers on China were misled into assuming that so massive a population must produce a massive foreign trade, once the country's doors were opened. But China's international trade has remained small. Even during the twenty-five years of unprecedented industrialization and modernization under the government of the People's Republic of China, China's foreign trade has never exceeded 2 percent of world trade. In 1974 it constituted 1.6 percent of world trade. Taiwan's was 1.5 percent. The purely economic impact of China's trade is therefore not large, except in a very few countries whose trade with China forms an exceptionally large part of their total foreign trade.

The economic impact of China's foreign trade is exceeded by its political impact. Although impossible to measure and difficult to disentangle from other influences, the political impact of the China trade has unquestionably been significant. During the PRC's long struggle for world recognition, the hope of expanding trade with China was one of the most influential arguments used by those favoring diplomatic relations with Peking. The PRC has sometimes supplemented this generalized lure of trade by deliberately withholding trade as a means of showing displeasure and exerting pressure. It has also, of course, like many other countries, used trade in the form of foreign aid to further its political purposes.

The Economic Impact of China's Trade

The only countries whose economies have been importantly dependent on trade with China are Albania, North Vietnam, North Korea, Hong Kong, and possibly Sri Lanka. Segments of the economies of certain countries, such as the wheat producers in Canada and Australia or the fertilizer and steel industries in Japan, rely on China as an important market, but the reliance is not such as to make the entire economy of any of these countries importantly dependent on the China trade. As for the other countries listed above, in 1968-69, 70 percent of Albania's trade was with the PRC, 25-40 percent of North Vietnam's and North Korea's, 12 percent of Sri Lanka's, and 9 percent of Hong Kong's. Only two other countries, Sudan and Singapore, had over 5 percent of their trade with China in that year.[1]

Of the three Communist countries, Albania remains the most dependent on the PRC economically and politically. Relations between Peking and Hanoi have cooled, and with the end of the Vietnam war Vietnam is is no longer so dependent as it was on shipments from China. It has expanded its trade relations with non-Communist states, notably Japan. North Korea also began several years ago to diversify its trade, but overextended itself and was caught by the world recession, unable to repay debts owed Japan and several Western European countries. It probably continues to be dependent on China for certain critical items, such as crude oil and petroleum products. Because of the Sino-Soviet dispute, however, both Hanoi and Pyongyang are in a position to play one of their larger partners off against the other, which inhibits Moscow and Peking from translating economic dependence into political leverage. Sri Lanka's trade with the PRC as a proportion of its total trade declined from 12 percent in 1968-69 to 8 percent in 1973.[2]

Hong Kong is in the unique position of being heavily dependent on China for foodstuffs and to some extent for water. Almost half of its food comes from China, as well as large amounts of raw materials for its export industries and a variety of textiles and other inexpensive consumer goods.[3] Although China as of 1974 supplied only 17 percent of Hong Kong's total imports,[4] the portion it does supply is vital to the subsistence of the population. It could be obtained from other sources, but only at considerably higher prices. Hong Kong's dependence on China is balanced, however, by China's dependence on Hong Kong. Because Hong Kong's exports to China are negligible, Hong Kong has been an indispensable source of hard currency for the PRC, in some years providing nearly one-third of its requirements.[5]

Even though the direct impact of China's trade on the economies of other countries is small, does it have an indirect impact in the form of the competition its goods may pose to countries exporting similar products? It has sometimes been predicted that China's low wages would enable it to dominate the markets of the world in the export of certain labor-intensive consumer goods. A study of the competitive impact of China's exports is beyond the scope of this chapter. But one significant example suggests that so far the problem is not serious. The leading manufactured export for both China and Taiwan is textile products. In 1973 China exported $1 billion, constituting 22 percent of its total exports, while Taiwan exported $1.3 billion, or approximately 28 percent of its total exports. Taiwan's exports of textile products to the United States, its largest market, were $368 million, while PRC exports amounted to only $2.1 million, increasing to $6.9 million in 1974, hardly a significant threat.[6] The ability of the PRC to penetrate the U.S. market would

improve somewhat if it were extended most-favored-nation
treatment, but other factors favoring Taiwan are probably
more important than this PRC disadvantage, including the
access that U.S. importers have to testile factories in
Taiwan, the ability of producers in Taiwan to meet buyers'
specifications as to style, brand name, etc., and to meet
tight time schedules, and in general the greater flexibility offered by Taiwan's free enterprise system. The same
advantages also protect other textile producers in East
Asia, such as Hong Kong and South Korea, from serious
PRC competition, at least in the markets of the large
industrial nations.

       The Political Impact of China's Trade: Japan

Trade has had a greater political impact on Japan than on
any of China's other trading partners for a variety of
reasons, including the attitude of the Japanese toward China,
the great importance of foreign trade to Japan's security
and prosperity, and the nature of the domestic political
balance in Japan.
       The Japanese have always felt a special closeness to
China, from which they obtained their written language and
which had a strong influence on many aspects of Japanese
culture. Since World War II the Japanese have harbored a
sense of guilt for their military aggression against China
and have been restive under the abnormal situation imposed
by their reliance on the United States for security and
economic growth which prevented them, up to 1972, from
having normal diplomatic relations with the PRC. The great
majority of Japanese felt that Japan should have a friendly
relation with China, especially after it became a nuclear
power, because the war experience had instilled in the
Japanese a deep resolve to avoid any future resort to
military force in their relations with their neighbors.
       Japan's situation was complicated, also, by its rela-
tions with the government of the Republic of China on
Taiwan. Many special relationships between Japanese and
the people of Taiwan had been created during the fifty
years the island was under Japanese control, and the
Japanese government had an interest in continuing close
relations with Taiwan for economic and strategic reasons
of its own, as well as to maintain cordial relations with
the United States, which strongly backed the Republic of
China.
       Living in an island state with few resources of its
own and having experienced the severance in war of its
economic lifelines to the outside, the Japanese are
unusually conscious of the importance of foreign trade

to their well-being. In Japan, as elsewhere, there was a
tendency to exaggerate the prospects for trade with China.
The PRC was able to exploit the high value the Japanese
attached to the China trade in order to gain political
advantage.

The deep division between left and right in Japanese
domestic politics facilitated Chinese efforts to exert
political leverage through trade. The principal opposition parties, the Japanese Socialist party (JSP) and the
Japanese Communist party (JCP), were both strongly anti-
American, pro-Chinese, and--to a lesser extent--pro-
Soviet, at least until the differences within the Communist
movement caused divisions between the JCP and the Communist
parties of the two large Communist states. The frequently
critical attitude of the media and of the Japanese intellectual community toward the security treaty with the United
States and government policies that could be attacked as
"subservient" to the United States placed the government on
the defensive and strengthened Chinese efforts to make
political gains through manipulating trade.

The Japanese government was buffeted by conflicting
currents: its need for good relations with the United
States; the insistent demands, even within the ruling party
itself, for closer relations with China; the need to prevent
the opposition from capitalizing on these demands; the
pressures on Tokyo from Taipei to reject any significant
concessions to Peking; and, as the Sino-Soviet dispute grew
more bitter, the need to strike a balance in relations
between Moscow and Peking, so as to avoid seeming to take
sides. The government attempted to disengage the China
trade from the issue of political relations with the PRC
by insisting on the principle of the separation of economics and politics, but Peking, which insisted on their
inseparability, succeeded in a variety of ways in linking
the two. Consequently, despite the Japanese government's
expressed desire to separate economics and politics, by the
late 1960s Japan's trade with China had a stronger political
coloration than that of any of China's other trading
partners.

The crudest attempt by the PRC to gain political advantage from manipulating trade occurred in 1958. A Japanese
delegation of Diet members and business leaders signed a
joint memorandum in Peking according the Chinese the right
to fly the PRC flag over a trade office to be established
in Tokyo. Japanese Foreign Minister Fujiyama insisted on
deleting this clause, which would have conferred a degree
of political status on the PRC that both Taipei and
Washington opposed. While negotiations for compromise continued, a young Japanse rightist tore down a small PRC
flag flying over a stamp exhibit in Nagasaki. Peking,
already irritated by a visit to Chiang Kai-shek by

Prime Minister Kishi, seized on the incident to condemn
the Kishi government and break off existing trade arrangements with Japan. Chinese leaders apparently misjudged
the balance of political forces within Japan and expected
the harsh action to be more effective than it was in gaining political concessions. The principal effect was to reduce trade between Japan and China to a very low level for
several years. It was not restored to the 1957 level until
1964.

When the Chinese, under pressure from the failure of
the Great Leap Forward and the break with the Soviet Union,
desired to restore trade with Japan, Chou En-lai announced
the conditions under which trade would take place: (1) a
governmental trade agreement based on the "three political
principles" should be concluded between China and Japan;
(2) even in the absence of a governmental agreement, private
transactions would be permitted; and (3) the practice of
giving special consideration to certain individual cases
of Japan-China trade would be continued. The three political principles stipulated that Japan must not adopt a
hostile attitude toward China, must not join in any
conspiracy to create two Chinas, and must not hinder the
normalization of Sino-Japanese relations.[7]

The Japanese government declined to conclude a governmental agreement with the PRC. Instead, in 1962 it sent a
Japanese politician with long experience in China,
Tatsunosuke Takasaki, to conclude a "private" agreement
with Liao Ch'eng-chih. Trade conducted within the framework
of this and subsequent similar agreements was first known
as Liao-Takasaki trade and later as "memorandum" trade.
This series of agreements, which provided for an exchange
of trade offices between the two countries, was negotiated
by politicians or business men, not by government officials,
but with the blessing and close collaboration of the
Japanese government. A separate agreement in 1964 provided
for an exchange of journalists between Peking and Tokyo.

The PRC has, on occasion, used the annual visits to
Peking by Japanese delegations to renew the trade agreements as a means of exerting political pressure on the
Japanese government. Particularly after Prime Minister
Sato in the Nixon-Sato communiqué of November 1969 under-
lined the importance to Japanese security of the security
of South Korea and the Taiwan area, the Chinese demanded
the insertion of statements critical of the policies of
the Japanese government in the joint communiqués issued
when new trade agreements were signed. By these tactics
and by delaying agreement to the annual negotiating ses-
sions, the PRC tried to stimulate anxiety among the
Japanese, implying that the continuance and expansion of
trade depended on conciliatory political behavior toward
China by the Japanese government. Gains to China through

the use of such tactics may well have been outweighed, however, by the irritation they caused within the ruling Liberal Democratic party (LDP).

A less formal type of trade between Japan and China, which the Japanese government tolerated but did not encourage directly as it did memorandum trade, was that carried on by a large number of so-called friendly firms. To qualify to conduct trade with China, firms had to demonstrate a friendly attitude toward the PRC. Thus, when left-wing groups in Japan organized demonstrations in favor of normalization of relations with the PRC or in opposition to the security treaty with the United States, they could count on the participation of and financial assistance from "friendly firms." Such firms also helped to finance the activities of the JCP up to the time it broke with the Chinese Communist Party.

In the spring of 1970 PRC attitude toward trade with Japan hardened, coincidental with a vociferous propaganda campaign against the alleged "revival of Japanese militarism." The negotiations on a new memorandum trade agreement were prolonged and difficult. Agreement was reached only when the head of the Japanese delegation, Yoshimi Furui, a member of the LDP, agreed to join the Chinese in a strong attack on the position taken by Prime Minister Sato in the Nixon-Sato communiqué and pledged to "resolutely oppose the Sato government's policy of hostility towards China."[8] A far more vituperative statement, incorporating wholesale the PRC's propaganda line against the Japanese government at that time, was signed by delegates from seven Japanese organizations representing "friendly firms."[9] These Japanese delegates even accepted the Chinese charges, rejected by the great majority of Japanese, that under Sato the revival of Japanese militarism was no longer just a threat, but had become a reality.

Chinese pressure on the Japanese members of the trade delegation to take positions so strongly critical of the Japanese government was widely resented in Japan, and Furui was bitterly criticized by some of his more conservative colleagues in the LDP. But Prime Minister Sato swallowed hard, attributed the Chinese attitude to misunderstanding, and publicly thanked Furui for his trouble.[10] Continuation of the trade "pipeline" with the PRC was so important to Japan that Chinese political pressure had to be endured.

The Chinese not only intensified their pressure against the Japanese government in the spring of 1970 but set political conditions for trade with China by Japanese firms, a step China had not taken toward the firms of any other country. Chou En-lai, in a meeting with Japanese delegates and other Japanese visitors following the signing of the memorandum trade agreement and issuance of the joint

communiqué, laid down four "principles" for Japanese firms
to observe in order to trade with China. He said that
China would not trade with (1) those wanting to help South
Korea and Taiwan, (2) those investing in enterprises in
South Korea or Taiwan, (3) those sending arms to aid the
United States in the wars in Vietnam and Cambodia, or
(4) U.S. enterprises in Japan.[11] Chou said that China would
cancel contracts with firms engaged in either memorandum
trade or "friendly firm" trade which violated these principles.

Japanese firms were much worried by the threat of PRC
sanctions against them for trading with or investing in
South Korea or Taiwan. Some of them informed the Chinese
that they would accept the four principles. Toyota with-
drew from a planned investment in South Korea, and other
Japanese companies refrained from increasing their investments either there or in Taiwan. An avalanche of further
acceptances of the Chou principles followed the surprise
announcement in July 1971 of President Nixon's plan to
visit China. Japanese companies feared American competition and did not want to be excluded from the China market
because of ties with South Korea or Taiwan.

Taking advantage of the "Nixon shock" to the Japanese
government and people, the Chinese redoubled their efforts
to add to rising pressures on the Japanese government to
accord diplomatic recognition to the PRC. The joint communiqué of the memorandum trade negotiators in March 1971
had again contained strong language, subscribed to by the
Japanese delegation, condemning the policies of the Sato
government and pledging the members of the delegation to
make new efforts to promote the restoration of diplomatic
relations between the two countries.[12] Pai Hsiang-kuo,
PRC minister of foreign trade, warned a high-level
Japanese trade delegation in September 1971 that only
after diplomatic relations were restored could conditions
favoring the healthy development of trade relations be
established.[13]

Another specific example of political influence exerted
on the Japanese by Chinese trade policy was the discourage-
ment of large Japanese investments in the development of
petroleum deposits in Siberia by holding out the prospect
of large crude oil exports from China to Japan. The political leverage derived from the offer of oil to Japan was
probably a secondary factor, both in the Chinese decision
to make the offer and the Japanese decision not to proceed
with investment in Siberian oil development; yet it was
unquestionably a consideration in the minds of both Chinese
and Japanese.

As early as 1966 the Soviets and Japanese had begun
discussion of Japanese investment in a pipeline to bring

oil from the Tyumen fields in western Siberia to the
Pacific coast to be exported to Japan. In February 1972
the Soviets made specific proposals for Japanese cooperation in the development of the Tyumen fields and the construction of a pipeline that would be able to supply Japan
with 25 to 50 million tons of oil annually for twenty years.
     Late that same year the Chinese first indicated a
willingness to export oil to Japan, after having for many
years discouraged Japanese hopes for Chinese oil by assert-
ing that China would not export its natural resources.
There were important economic reasons for the Chinese change
of policy at this time, for the PRC had decided to import
western plants and machinery on a large scale and oil was
the only product whose export could be quickly stepped up
to pay for the increased imports. That political considerations were also involved, however, was suggested by Liao
Ch'eng-chih's warning to the Japanese in March 1973 that
the Chinese would be "bitter" toward the Japanese if they
went ahead with the Tyumen project, which he said would
significantly strengthen Soviet military forces confronting China.[14] Chinese projections of oil exports of 30 to
50 million tons by 1980 with no Japanese investment required
were clearly more attractive than a Soviet proposal for
Japanese investment of several billion dollars to produce
an annual export by 1985 which the Soviets had cut back
from their initial offer of a maximum of 40 million tons
to only 25 million. The ultimate Japanese decision to
shelve the Tyumen project, although influenced by Chinese
pressures and inducements, was probably based primarily on
the failure of the United States to join in the project
and changes made by the Soviets in their original proposal,
including reducing the export target, increasing the
Japanese investment required, and deciding to build a
second trans-Siberian railway to transport the oil part
of the way.

The Political Impact of China's Trade: West Germany and
Canada

Studies of the politics and economics of China's trade
with the Federal Republic of Germany and Canada show how
inextricably these two aspects of international relations
are intertwined.[15] Initially, trade was limited by
political factors; it failed to reach the level it might
have reached if economics alone had governed the exchange.
But the desire to expand trade with China in both western
countries exerted continuing pressure on the governments
to lower the political barriers.
     For its part, Peking wanted trade with Canada and West
Germany for both economic and political reasons. It never

halted or threatened to cut off trade as a means of putting
political pressure on the Canadian or West German governments as it had done with Japan. Neither were Canadian
and German businessmen visiting China required to attack
publicly the policies of their own governments toward the
PRC. Chinese officials probably recognized that Western
governments and businessmen would be more resistant than
the Japanese to Chinese efforts to link trade and politics.
     Peking did, however, in a more subtle fashion than
in its relations with Japan manipulate trade to improve its
political position. For example, in negotiations with
German traders in the mid-1950s, the Chinese at first
insisted that trade between the two countries would require
a government-to-government agreement. For Bonn such an
agreement was out of the question because of the opposition
of the United States--the Federal Republic's relations with
the United States were far more important than its relations
with China. Consequently, the Chinese finally backed away
from their insistence on an official agreement and an agreement was worked out in 1957 between the China Committee of
the Ostausschuss der Deutschen Wirtschaft (Committee of
German Industry on Trade with the East), a "private"
organization closely collaborating with the German government, and the China Council for the Promotion of International Trade (CCPIT).[16] In the same year, despite the
displeasure of the United States, the Germans followed the
British lead in dropping the so-called China differential
on trade with China, bringing restrictions on the shipment
of strategic goods to China in line with those applied to
the USSR. Thus, Peking handled its trade negotiations with
Bonn so as to produce small but significant political
dividends.
     In negotiations in 1964 the Chinese renewed their
demand for a formal trade treaty. They also expressed
interest in liberalized credits and in the exchange of
trade exhibits and permanent trade missions. The Germans
were interested, for they were seeking international recognition at this time that West Berlin was an integral part
of the Federal Republic and would like to have inserted a
"Berlin clause" in an agreement with China. But the United
States strongly opposed any formal trade agreement and the
Chinese would not accept an informal one, so the negotiations broke down. One political advance in relations
between the two nations did take place in that year,
however, an agreement on the exchange of journalists,
which may have been facilitated by the interest both sides
had in expanding trade.
     After 1964 Sino-German trade increased and the Chinese
refrained from further attempts to use it for political
advantage. As the Sino-Soviet dispute became sharper,
concern in Bonn at the possible Soviet reaction to

improvement in political relations with Peking added to
Bonn's concern over U.S. reactions. The increased political sensitivity of all parties to this complex international equation probably reduced possibilities for effective use of trade as leverage. In fact, the principal
feature of Sino-German trade is the fact that it was sustained at substantial levels despite formidable political
obstacles. Efforts by either the Chinese or the Germans
to place on trade the burden of achieving important political advantages might easily have overloaded the circuit
and ended by diminishing trade instead of accomplishing
the political objectives.

The political impact of the China trade appears to
have been somewhat greater in Canada than in Germany
because of the peculiar importance of wheat in the
Canadian economy and the political influence of wheat
growers and the West Coast shipping interests that benefited from large wheat sales to China. Canadian exports
to China never exceeded 2.3 percent of its total exports
and in some years were much less, but in 1962 they accounted
for 25 percent of all Canadian wheat exports and subsequently varied from 12 to 17 percent.[17] Consequently, the
China market became important to those sections of Canada
dependent on wheat, especially in the years when the market for wheat was depressed and the government was
accumulating large surpluses.

Although the Canadian government did not enter into
a formal government-to-government trade agreement with the
PRC, the wheat trade inevitably required substantial
government involvement. The Wheat Board, which negotiated
the sales, was under the direct supervision of a government
minister. Moreover, in order to grant the favorable credit
arrangements pressed for by the Chinese, the government
had to extend guarantees. The extent of government involvement provided grounds for politicians responsible for
initiating sales to China to claim political credit. And
the importance of the issue to a substantial segment of
voters in key regions meant that any politician not fully
backing government promotion of wheat sales to China would
risk serious loss of support.

Canada's China trade also affected and was affected
by Canadian-U.S. relations. On the one hand, the United
States discouraged trade with China by Canadian subsidiaries
of U.S. companies. While this U.S. attitude probably did
not greatly diminish the opportunities that Canadian
industry might otherwise have had to export to China, it
did excite Canadian nationalism and confer on the China
trade a symbolic importance as a manifestation of Canadian
independence from U.S. dictation which provided useful
campaign material for Canadian politicians.

Canadian motivations for recognizing the PRC in 1970

were varied. Henry S. Albinski and F. Conrad Raabe judged
trade to be "incidental but not irrelevant."[18] The Chinese
had from time to time intimated that improved political
relations would result in increased trade, but they never
threatened to withhold trade as a means of applying direct
political pressure on this issue. In a nation in which
the importance of foreign trade to the economy was generally
recognized and where wheat was a leading export, the climate
of opinion naturally approved actions that favored the continued or expanded exportation of wheat, but broader considerations seem to have been more important than trade
in the minds of Canadian policymakers when they decided
to recognize the PRC.

The PRC took advantage of Canadian recognition to place
pressure on Australia--which had not recognized it--by
withholding trade. The Chinese failed to make their cus-
tomary wheat purchases from Australia in 1970-71 and let
it be known that Australians could not expect commercial
treatment as favorable as that extended to Canada so long
as Australia declined to recognize the PRC or support its
seating in the United Nations. This Chinese pressure
produced a more conciliatory attitude toward the PRC on
the part of the Australian government.

Political Influence through Foreign Economic Aid

China, like many other nations, has sought to improve its
relations with developing countries by extending economic
aid, principally to states in Africa and South Asia. From
1956 to 1974 it made commitments totaling $3.5 billion,
over two-thirds of this amount in the 1970s.[19] These
commitments averaged slightly under $500 million annually
from 1970 to 1974. In the peak year, 1970, economic aid
commitments were equivalent to 34 percent of the PRC's
exports, but by 1974 they had fallen off to 4 percent.
Of course, deliveries on commitments were stretched out
over a period of several years after the commitments were
made. Nevertheless, the PRC's foreign economic aid program
has been substantial in proportion to its relatively
small export trade.

Political influence gained through economic aid
programs cannot, of course, be measured. The United States
and the USSR have found over the years that influence
obtained by this means is transitory. The PRC, although
unable to compete with the superpowers or even Japan in
volume of foreign aid, appears to have been relatively
successful in creating a favorable impression among the
recipients. Credit terms for Chinese aid are generous,
the grant component of aid is comparatively large, and
PRC technicians are willing to live at the same spartan

level as the average citizen in the developing country
being aided.

The Future International Impact of China's Trade

Now that most nations of the world have established diplomatic relations with the PRC, its scope for manipulating trade
for political advantage has been reduced. The United
States is one of the few countries left to which the PRC
can hold out the prospect for larger trade in exchange for
diplomatic recognition. But the political pressures that
can be generated in the United States by this means are
minor, for even the most optimistic estimates do not see
China becoming a major trading partner of the United
States in the foreseeable future.
     The international impact of China's trade could, of
course, increase substantially if the post-Mao leadership
in China should decide to rely more heavily on foreign
trade than in the past to speed economic development. A
decision, for example, to solicit long-term credits, as
the Soviet Union has, in order to import foreign technology would lead to the rapid expansion of China's foreign
trade. If the PRC were to enter into production-sharing
arrangements with American oil companies for the exploitation of undersea oil resources off China, the production
and export of oil could be increased more rapidly. The
denunciation of the Gang of Four and Hua Kuo-feng's
appointment as Mao's successor as chairman of the Chinese
Communist Party have improved prospects for expansion of
China's foreign trade, but it remains to be seen whether
such far-reaching innovations as long-term loans or
foreign participation in the production of Chinese oil
will be adopted.
     Should China's foreign trade increase during the next
ten years more rapidly than world trade, its general
economic impact would increase to that extent. But increasing involvement in international trade seems likely to
reduce rather than increase Chinese attempts to manipulate
trade for political ends. For the more the Chinese economy
becomes dependent on the world economy, the higher the
economic cost of manipulating trade for purely political
purposes. Bureaucratic reluctance to pay such costs is
likely to grow stronger and could be overcome only by
strong leaders less concerned than the bureaucracy with
the growth of China's economy and more concerned with
international political goals.
     The political goal for which Chinese leaders might
be most willing to incur economic costs during the next
ten years is the "liberation" of Taiwan. Chou En-Lai's
"four principles" were an example of the kind of measures

the PRC might resort to again in order to put pressure
on Taiwan. The island is extraordinarily dependent on
foreign trade to maintain its thriving economy and high
rate of economic growth; in recent years exports have
constituted close to 50 percent of GNP. The PRC may be
tempted to exploit this vulnerability by compelling
foreign firms to choose between trade with the PRC and
trade with Taiwan. But unless China greatly increases
its foreign trade, the leverage it could exert in this
manner is not great. Taiwan's two-way foreign trade
was only slightly below that of the PRC in 1974, and for
many foreign companies Taiwan is a more promising market
or a more dependable source of supply than the PRC. And
there are innumerable ways by which foreign firms could
evade the PRC's conditions, as Japanese firms learned
in coping with Chou's principles.
     A substantial increase in the PRC's foreign trade
could affect other aspects of its foreign policy. For
example, the more important foreign trade becomes to the
PRC, the greater its stake in a stable world environment
in which that trade could prosper. Trade also serves as
an important means of institutionalizing bilateral relations with other countries, particularly those with
which the PRC has not yet established diplomatic relations, such as the United States and Singapore. PRC
trade with Southeast Asian countries reinforces the
PRC's political influence in those countries. But it
may also inhibit the PRC from supporting Communist sub-
version and insurgency in those countries, for the
balance of trade in the region heavily favors the PRC.
Consequently, Peking might hesitate to take actions
that would jeopardize significant flows of hard currency
from those countries, especially from Malaysia and
Singapore.

                         Notes

     1.   Audrey Donnithorne, "China as a Trading Nation,"
Current Scene, February 7, 1972, pp. 2-3; International
Monetary Fund, Direction of Trade Annual, 1968-72, pp.
254-55.
     2.   International Monetary Fund, Direction of Trade
Annual, 1969-73, p. 259.
     3.   Colina MacDougall Lupton, "Hong Kong's Role in
Sino-Western Trade" in Arthur A. Stahnke, ed., China's
Trade with the West: A Political and Economic Analysis
(New York: Praeger, 1972), p. 196.
     4.   Direction of Trade, Jan. 1976, pp. 55-56.
     5.   Lupton, p. 189.
     6.   William Clarke and Martha Avery, "The Sino-

American Commercial Relationship" in <u>China: A Reassess-</u>
<u>ment of the Economy</u>, Joint Economic Committee, U.S.
Congress (Washington, D.C.: U.S. Government Printing
Office, 1975), p. 514; Nai-Ruenn Chen, "China's Foreign
Trade, 1950-74," ibid., p. 647; Economic Planning Coun-
cil, Republic of China, <u>Taiwan Statistical Data Book</u>,
<u>1975</u>, pp. 190, 196.
    7. Japanese Ministry of Foreign Affairs, "The
Present State of Japan-China Trade," <u>Current Scene</u>.
May 1, 1970, p. 8. The text of Chou's statement was
carried by the New China News Agency on Sept. 12, 1960.
    8. Foreign Broadcast Information Service (FBIS),
<u>Daily Report: Communist China</u>, April 20, 1970, pp.
A7-A12.
    9. Ibid., April 15, 1970, pp. A3-A6.
    10. <u>Asahi</u>, evening ed., April 20, 1970.
    11. Kyodo, April 20, 1970, in FBIS, <u>Daily Report:</u>
<u>Communist China</u>, April 20, 1970, p. A11. The four con-
ditions were spelled out more precisely in the joint
communiqué issued by the memorandum trade representatives
of the two countries on March 1, 1971, which said that
the Chinese would not trade with (1) factories and firms
helping the Chiang Kai-shek gang stage a comeback to the
mainland or helping the Chung Hee Park clique intrude
into the Democratic People's Republic of Korea;
(2) factories and firms with large investments in Taiwan
or South Korea; (3) enterprises supplying arms and am-
munition to U.S. imperialism for aggression against
Vietnam, Laos, or Cambodia; and (4) U.S.-Japan joint
enterprises or subsidiaries of U.S. companies in Japan
(<u>Mainichi</u>, English ed., March 3, 1971).
    12. Ibid.
    13. FBIS, <u>Daily Report: People's Republic of</u>
<u>China</u>, Sept. 23, 1971, p. A14.
    14. <u>Yomiuri</u>, March 12, 1973.
    15. The discussion that follows draws on Arthur A.
Stahnke, "The Political Context of Sino-West German Trade"
and Henry S. Albinski and F. Conrad Raabe, "Canada's
Chinese Trade in Political Perspective" in Stahnke, ed.,
<u>China's Trade with the West</u>.
    16. As a private organization engaged in trade
neogtiations with the CCPIT with the blessing of its
government, the Ostausschuss was an early forerunner of
the National Council for the Promotion of U.S.-China
Trade in the United States.
    17. Albinski and Raabe, p. 92.
    18. Ibid., p. 122.
    19. Bureau of Intelligence and Research, Department
of State, <u>Communist States and Developing Countries: Aid</u>
<u>and Trade in 1974</u>, Jan. 27, 1976, Table 4.

About the Editor and the Contributors

Nai-ruenn Chen is Economist in the Bureau of East-West Trade, U.S. Department of Commerce. A former professor at Cornell, he is author of Chinese Economic Statistics (1967) and coauthor of The Chinese Economy Under Communism (1969).

Ralph N. Clough is a senior fellow of the Brookings Institution. As a U.S. foreign service officer, he was stationed in China and Taiwan for a number of years. He is author of East Asia and U.S. Security (1974) and coauthor of The United States, China, and Arms Control (1975).

Jerome A. Cohen is Professor of Law, Director of East Asian Legal Studies, and Associate Dean, Harvard Law School. He is the author and editor of many books on China, the latest being the prizewinning People's China and International Law (1974).

Robert F. Dernberger is Professor of Economics at the University of Michigan. He has written extensively on Chinese economy. Among his publications are China Trade and U.S. Policy (1971) (coauthorship) and China's Future (1977), also coauthorship.

Tao-tai Hsia is Chief of the Far Eastern Law Division of the Library of Congress. He has published many works on Chinese law, including The 1975 Revised Constitution of the People's Republic of China (1975).

Shao-chuan Leng is Doherty Foundation Professor of Government and Chairman of the Asian Studies Committee at the University of Virginia. Among his recent publications are Justice in Communist China: A Survey of the Judicial System in the Chinese People's Republic (1967) and Law in Chinese Foreign Policy (1972), ed. and contrib.

Choon-ho Park is a research fellow of East Asian Legal Studies at Harvard Law School. He has published a number of articles on the law of the sea.

Robert A. Scalapino is Professor of Political Science at the University of California, Berkeley, Director of its East Asian Center, and editor of Asian Survey. He has written extensively on China, Japan, Korea, and U.S.-Asian policy. Among his recent works are Political Elites in the People's Republic of China (1972), ed. and contrib.; Asia and the Road Ahead (1975); and The Foreign Policy of Modern Japan (1977), ed. and contrib.

Eugene A. Theroux is a partner in the law firm of Baker & McKenzie, Washington, D.C. Past Vice-President of the

National Council for U.S.-China Trade, he has made ten visits to the PRC and has written numerous articles on the business and legal aspects of trade with China.